TO STANLEY KUNITZ, WITH LOVE
From Poet Friends

for his 96th birthday

*To Pete Gunn,
with Love*

From a Poet Friend

for his 70th birthday

THE SHEEP MEADOW PRESS
RIVERDALE-ON-HUDSON, NEW YORK

love, Naveer Martin

All inquiries and permission requests should be addressed to:
The Sheep Meadow Press
PO Box 1345
Riverdale-on-Hudson, NY 10471

Cover photo by Joel Meyerowitz

Designed and typeset by S.M.
Distributed by The University Press of New England.

Printed on acid-free paper in the United States. This book meets the guidelines for permanence and durability of the Committee on Production Guidelines for Book Longevity of the Council on Library Resources.

Library of Congress Cataloging-in-Publication Data

A tribute to Stanley Kunitz on his ninety-sixth birthday / edited by Stanley Moss
       p. cm.
  ISBN 1-878818-92-9 (alk. paper)
   1. Kunitz, Stanley, 1905---Appreciation. 2. Poets, American--20th century--Biography.
3. Kunitz, Stanley, 1905---Poetry. 4. Poetry, modern--20th century.

PS3521.U7 Z88 2001
810.8'0351--dc21   2001042625

TO STANLEY KUNITZ, WITH LOVE
FROM POET FRIENDS

CONTENTS

Galway Kinnell
Daybreak   1

Gerald Stern
Two Daws   2
American Heaven   6

Stanley Plumly
Kunitz Tending Roses   7
Reading With The Poets   9

Susan Mitchell
A Visit to the Poet's Studio   11
Lost Parrot   26

Robert Bly
With Love For Stanley   28

Seamus Heaney
The Boiling House   29

W.S. Merwin
Letter of April 18, 2001   30
To Impatience   31

Richard Wilbur
Dear Stanley   33

Tory Dent
When Atheists Pray   34

Yusef Komunyakaa
Blessing The Animals   45
Providence   47
The Song Thief   50

Maxine Kumin
For Stanley, Some Lines At Random 51

Louise Glück
Four Dreams Concerning The Master 52

Kenneth Koch
For Stanley 54

Carolyn Kizer
The Animal Master 55

Sharon Olds
Meditation on "The Portrait" 57

Stanley Moss
A History Of Color 59
Song For Stanley Kunitz 65

Lucille Clifton
flowers 67
if i stand in my window 68

Mary Oliver
Snowy Night 69

Reetika Vazirani
Letter To The Moor 71
English 73
Beijing 75

Paul Muldoon
Hard Drive 76

Cleopatra Mathis
Old Trick 77
Cutlery 78
What To Tip The Boatman? 80

Bruce Smith
Sweets   82
White Girl, Alabama   83

Gail Mazur
Dana Street, December   86

Peter Balakian
Photosynthesis   89

Grace Schulman
Blue Dawn   91
In The Café   92
Poem Ending With A Phrase From The Psalms   93

Michael Ryan
Reminder   94
Every Sunday   95

Elise Asher
Cycle   96
Walkng After A Rainstorm   97

Dannie Abse
Snapshot Of Ruskin In Venice   98
Fly   100

Stephen Berg
Fleas   101
Like Singing   102
*   103

Mark Rudman
Bicoastal: Bobby Darin At The Copa   104

Peter Davison
Tasting The Fire   106

Hugh Seidman
Somebody Stand Up And Sing   108

Diana Der-Hovanessian
Tell The Armenian Story   110

Alberto Ríos
Small Risings   112

Christopher Middleton
An Image In The Hatch   113

Forrest Gander
To The Invisible World   115

Anne Marie Macari
Slope Of Stone And Dirt   117

Arthur Gregor
Portrait   119

Joshua Weiner
Psalm   122

Bodhan Boychuck
After Reading "Hornworm"   125

Shirley Kaufman
A Sheet Of Foil   126
All over Rehavia there are   128

Allison Funk
Heart's-ease   130

Nick Flynn
Inside Nothing   132

Gregory Orr
Be-All   134

Tess Gallagher
Behave   135

Alan Dugan
Jewels of Indoor Glass   136
The Dark Tower   137
On Looking For Models   138

Contributors' Notes   141

Authors' royalties and any profit to the publisher will go to the Provincetown Work Center.

To Stanley Kunitz, With Love

Galway Kinnell

DAYBREAK

On the tidal mud, just before sunset,
dozens of starfishes
were creeping. It was
as though the mud were a sky
and enormous, imperfect stars
moved across it as slowly
as the actual stars cross heaven.
All at once they stopped,
and, as if they had simply
increased their receptivity
to gravity, they sank down
into the mud, faded down
into it and lay still, and by the time
pink of sunset broke across them
they were as invisible
as the true stars at daybreak.

*To Stanley,
with love,
Galway*

Gerald Stern

TWO DAWS

The false dawn in Wheeling, West Virginia
is five o'clock—given the season—given
the inclination of two or three daws to sing
outside my frozen room; there is some fog,
there is some light; the birds go back to sleep
then, something like I do, waking themselves I'm sure
just as I do with something of a snort
when finicky memory combines with green sulphur—
in their case maybe it's vile hunger combining
with cold, slightly different. I call it "false" dawn
as if it were a fixture; I will talk
to two or three others, a sweet librarian,
a morose poet; I always check to see
if there is a cosmos to match my own. I learned
thirty years ago how odd my thoughts were,
how I could not be trusted. If *I* described
the morning I would say there are two dawns,
one, if it's late April, if it's in the East,
it's night still, there is a kind of thin blue
over the hills; and, two, the true dawn, then
the trees are almost shaking with noise, the sun
is spread out, light is everywhere. There are
two deaths as well—though I will have to check it—
false death, there is a bird then, still a daw,
or sometimes a jay, depending on the season,
and the location; I think in West Virginia
it could be any of twenty birds, the cardinal
is good, the dove is good, they sing with such a
note—such notes—of pity my nose is red

from weeping, my eyes are swollen, there are creases
of woe in my forehead, I am dragging my feet
like never before, it is a sacrifice
and I am holding the knife; I want it to be
a stone knife—I can pick my weapon. The other
the birds are silent; I would have them screaming
and scolding, but I have no authority there.
Kunitz, may he live forever, says
there's only one dawn. It's like an orchestra,
first, say, a lark, or first a robin, and then
it's the finch's turn; maybe the flutes are first
and then the cellos and the flutes are silent.
That is the lull. We in the trombones slide
slowly, don't we—what a din we made.
But there are *two* deaths, he's wrong—only once—that gorgeous
poet, there are *two* deaths, though now I remember
he only spoke of "dawn," he didn't speak
of "death"—he never said there weren't two deaths—
I was the one who brought up those birds and had them
singing and scratching twice, he kept his counsel
on death, and everyone I talked to we reasoned
together about two "dawns," and almost everyone
said there were two, or they agreed with me
to show how smart they were or they just found
the thought intriguing. No one said there were,
or said there weren't, two deaths; I'm all alone
with my two deaths, I have to make my own birds
and my own cat, for that matter, sitting and watching
or walking slowly by with a flea collar
choking him, or dragging a bell from his throat.
—False dawn maybe is only a light birds are
fooled by, though the light could be from within,
triggered by fear—or hunger; I almost think it's
curiosity—which kills all birds. False death
is almost like it; light from something drags us

out, breathing our last, fresh blood pumping
through our necks and wrists, terror forcing us
down, last-minute cunning, last-minute hope
saving us—counting to ten, humming, laughing,
at what I called light—instead of darkness—knowing
more than I say—more than I can say—but true dawn—
ah sapsuckers singing from my birch, the branches
of my giant arbor vitae shaking, the needles
of my great yews dancing, not to mention the copper
beech, or the weeping willow, not to mention
the crab apple, not to mention the dying
redbud, not to mention the oak. The word
"dawn" it comes from the "daw," there has to be
some connection with the bird; "daw"
is middle English: "there are two daws"; "death"
is from old Frisian, that from old Saxon, that from
old High German. When it comes to true death
Kunitz is just like me, I guess, polite
and a little terrified, certainly amazed. I
have nothing to say about which birds; I think
of crows, naturally, although that should be false
death, shouldn't it? I say that with respect
for one soul and another. I think it's geese
I think about, walking with their webbed feet
down some greasy path, honking with caution,
almost with rudeness, yet lifting their huge bodies
and disappearing, in ten or twelve seconds, life
and death are in their rising and falling; swallows
are birds of death, in and out, trees
I won't get started on, either here, wherever
here is, or in the next place, or in the last place,
not one locust, not one cyprus. I
am full of spring these days, I listen to a hundred
sounds of shrieking every morning. Kunitz
is right about the orchestra—and yet,

isn't it reversed? Isn't true dawn
the one that is operatic? Shouldn't I sing then,
breathing my last, fretting over my own death
among the other birds? And shouldn't I sleep
like a wise man through the false dawn even if the first
thin blue is out there, even if there is a call
from one or two creatures, even if the cardinal
is making me moan, and even if the chickadee
is hanging upside down and banging his head
against the shiny glass—even if the worm
is fighting for his life and the lily of the valley
is bowing her head in shame, shouldn't I live on?

Gerald Stern

AMERICAN HEAVEN

A salt water pond in the Hamptons near David
Ignatow's house, the water up to my chest,
an American Heaven, a dog on the shore, this time
his mouth closed, his body alert, his ears
up, a dog *belongs* in heaven, at least our
kind. An egret skidding to a stop, I'm sure
water snakes and turtles, grasses and weeds,
and close to the water sycamores and locusts,
and pitch pine on the hill and sand in the distance,
and girls could suckle their babies standing in water,
so that was our place of origin, that was
the theory in 1982—David
had his own larder, Rose had hers, he brought
tuna fish into her kitchen, it was a triptych,
the center piece was the pond, the left panel
was his, his study, and he was stepping naked
across the frame into the pond holding an
open can and hers was the right, her arms had
entered the pond, holding a bowl, it was her
studio, we ate on a dry stone
and talked about James Wright and Stanley Kuntiz,
and there was a star of the fourth magnitude
surrounded by planets, shining on all of us.

Stanley Plumly

KUNITZ TENDING ROSES

Naturally he doesn't hear too well,
so that when he's kneeling he's really
listening at the very mouth of the flower.
And the feeling in his hands, his sense
of touch, seems gloved if not quite gone,
though when he bleeds he takes a certain
notice, wipes it away, then moves on.

And winter eyes. The old have passion's
winter eyes, which see with a pointillist
chill clarity, but must look close, as his do,
petal by petal, since the work is tactile
visual: Cadenza, Blaze, Red Fountain climbing
or like free-standing rhododendron,
sunset gold Medallion, scarlet Maiden.

His body bends depending on the height
and cluster or, on a perfect scale, the stature
of the rose, which, like the day, declines
continually: meaning that toward evening
he almost disappears among the fragrance,
gala, and double flesh of roses: or when
he's upright, back to the sun, is thin

enough to see through, thorn and bone.
Still, there he is, on any given day,
talking to ramblers, floribundas, Victorian
perpetuals, as if for beauty and to make us
glad or otherwise for envy and to make us

wish for more—if only to mystify and move us.
The damasked, dusky hundred-petaled heart.

Interrogate the rose, ask the old,
who have the seminal patience of flowers,
which question nothing, less for why we ask:
Enchanter, Ember, Blood Talisman, something
to summarize the color of desire, aureate
or red passion, something on fire to hold
in the hand, the hand torn with caring.

Stanley Plumly

READING WITH THE POETS

Whitman among the wounded, at the bedside,
kissing the blood off boys' faces, sometimes stilled
faces, writing their letters, writing the letters
home, saying, sometimes, the white prayers, helping,
sometimes, with the bodies or holding the bodies
down. The boy with the scar that cuts through his speech,
who's followed us here to the Elizabeth
Zane Memorial and Cemetery, wants
to speak nevertheless on the Civil War's
stone-scarred rows of dead and the battle here
just outside of Wheeling equal in death to
Gettysburg because no doctor between the war
and Pittsburgh was possible. Boys dressed like men

and men would gangrene first before the shock of
the saw and scalpel. Three days between this part
of the Ohio River and Pittsburgh. He
knows, he is here since then a child of history
and knows Elizabeth Zane saved all she could.
Keats all his wounded life wanted to be a healer,
which he was, once at his mother's bedside, failed,
once at his brother's, failed. Whitman in Washington
failed: how many nights on the watch and it broke
him, all those broken boys, all those bodies blessed
into the abyss. Now the poem for Lincoln,
now the boy with the scar almost singing, now
the oldest surviving poet of the war
reading one good line, then another, then
the song of the hermit thrush from the ground cover.

Lincoln's long black brooding body sailed in a train,
a train at the speed of the wind blossoming,
filling and unfilling the trees, a man's slow
running. Whitman had nowhere to go, so I
leave thee lilac with heart-shaped leaves, he says at
last, and went to the other side with the corpses,
myriads of them, soldiers' white skeletons,
far enough into the heart of the flower
that none of them suffered, none of them grieved, though
the living had built whole cities around them.

Keats at his medical lectures drew flowers.
Not from indifference, not from his elegance:
his interest couldn't bear the remarkable
screams of the demonstrations. He sat there, still
a boy, already broken, looking into the living
body, listening to the arias of the spirit
climbing. So the boy at the graves of the Union
singing, saying his vision, seeing the bodies
broken into the ground. Now the poem for Lincoln.
Now the oldest surviving poet still alive
weaving with the audience that gossamer,
that thread of the thing we find in the voice again.
Now in the night our faces kissed by the healer.

Susan Mitchell

A VISIT TO THE POET'S STUDIO

A couple of months ago during a long night of insomnia that seemed the price paid for my recent dislocation from New England to South Florida, I reread Dante's *Vita Nuova* and Stanley Kunitz's *Next-To-Last Things* (The Atlantic Monthly Press, 1985). It was not only the fact that, once again, I was starting my life over that returned me to Dante and, for that matter, to Kunitz, whose poems bear witness to his own powerful drive for spiritual renewal and transformation. I chose these writers because I had read them so often I knew they would give me an alternative to geographic place: they were a familiar intellectual soil I was already rooted in and a soil made all the more hospitable by my own numerous underlinings, asterisks, personal jottings penciled in margins. Here, said each marking, was a place I had stopped and thought and dreamed before. As I settled into that long reading, first one, then the other book spread open in my lap, the night itself opened around me. Nights in South Florida, I was to learn that night, are not really dark, but different shades of blue. When I glanced up from my reading, there was the swimming pool, clearly visible, an eerie pale blue in the artificial light of the courtyard; and beyond the swimming pool and the rustling date palms, a deep water canal, sometimes navy, sometimes a muddy violet — colors not so much seen as sensed whenever a rhythmic slap of waves against the dock signaled the passing of a boat on its way to the Intracoastal. My move to Florida had coincided with the start of the rainy season, and at intervals during that night, torrents of rain would suddenly gush, pummel, and pour in columns so thick it was hard to tell whether the rain was falling or growing up from the earth, stalactite or stalagmite — and then as abruptly as it had begun, the rain would stop. Sometimes a bird let fall long plumes of song, though with the source of the singing invisible, it seemed as if the air had become saturated with music, as well as with water, and at intervals had to spill down in trills and rivulets of song. Other times, birdsong arced, then dropped like a flare, the music momentarily illuminating the farthest reaches of the night: I was seeing all the way to the Keys where Florida trails off into dots and dashes — the geographic impulse tapering into archipelagoes, into the Dry Tortugas where the state finally dives into wild waters of the Atlantic or else lifts on a sudden updraft, soaring with the black frigate-birds above the last malarial outpost, Fort Jefferson, where Dr. Samuel Mudd, guilty of setting the broken leg of Lincoln's assassin, wrote long letters home to Maryland and his wife.

During that night I felt lost within the enormous flatness of Florida, a terrain so filled with water — lakes, swamps, inlets, rivers, irrigation canals — that from the air, much of the state appears in continual motion; and at the same time, I felt the proud possessor of a geography that seemed to contract as easily as it could expand: the state suddenly reduced to that hand-sized piece I loved to snap into the jigsaw puzzle map of the United States I was given for my ninth birthday — Florida, an exciting Benadryl pink against the deep wooden blue of the Atlantic. It was within this shifting terrain that I read *Next-To-Last Things*, a book which is itself unusually concerned with shape-lifting. "I will try to speak of the beauty of shapes," says Socrates in a passage from Plato's *Philebus* which provides the epigraph for the book's first section of thirteen poems. The shapes Socrates has in mind are the primal lineaments of the natural world and geometry: "straight lines and curves and the shapes made from them by the lathe, rules or square." With this passage, we are close to the Platonic notion of ideal forms, those primordial figures from which the concrete, sensuous world is copied. And with ideal forms, we are in the studio where creation begins.

What Henry James called "the sacred mystery of structure" has always been of crucial importance for Kunitz. Accumulative, circular, dialectical — these, he told his poetry workshop students at Columbia University, are the three basic patterns that shape meaning in poems. As Kunitz explained each fundamental pattern, I felt as if the keys to the universe had just been handed over to me. And, in a way, they had. For these structures inform not only works of art, but also the natural world, and are probably a part of the human brain in the way that the dark spot that draws the bee deep inside the flower is probably a part of the bee's eye. In *Next-To-Last Things*, shapes abound, sometimes as dimly felt presences:

Out there is childhood country,
bleached faces peering in
with coals for eyes.
("The Abduction")

other times as distinct, recognizable forms:

On the back door screen
a heavy furpiece hangs,
spreadeagled, breathing hard,
hooked by prehensile fingers,
with its pointed snout pressing in,
and the dark agates of its bandit eyes
furiously blazing. Behind,
where shadows deepen, burly forms
lumber from side to side
("Raccoon Journal")

But it is not the shapes of living figures, or even the shapes of phantasms, that preoccupy Kunitz in this book. What fascinates him is the shape of human consciousness, the shifting shapes of the poet's mind at work, its "rush of forms" — that place of becoming I think of as the poet's studio.

As early as his first book, *Intellectual Things* (1930), Kunitz was concerned with mind, and in a tightly packed sonnet, entitled "Organic Bloom," he expressed three ideas which were to turn up again and again in his work, though it is only now in *Next-To-Last Things* that these ideas are fully explored. Listen, first, to the early sonnet:

The brain constructs its systems to enclose
The steady paradox of thought and sense;
Momentously its tissued meaning grows
To solve and integrate experience.
But life escapes closed reason. We explain
Out chaos into cosmos, cell by cell,
Only to learn of some insidious pain
Beyond the limits of our chartered hell,
A guilt not mentioned in our prayers, a sin
Conceived against the self. So, vast and vaster
The plasmic circles of gray discipline
Spread outward to include each new disaster.
Enormous floats the brain's organic bloom
Till, bursting like a fruit, it scatters doom.

To begin with, this sonnet shows Kunitz attempting to find visual shapes for mental processes. In another poem from the same book, "This Very Tree," Kunitz speaks of "the candelabrum of pure thought," and in still another, "Mens Creatrix," he writes, "Brain, be ice, / A frozen bowl of thought." Secondly, "Organic Bloom" shows Kunitz connecting processing of thought with organic processes that work on cycles: like fruit, the thinking processes appear to ripen — then burst. In another poem from *Intellectual Things*, "Motion of Wish," the wish, which is "sprung from the brain," goes "through evolutions of the seed." Like the Creation of the Lurianic Kabbalah which works on a triple rhythm of contracting, bursting apart, and healing, the creative process for Kunitz is combustive, culminating in explosion. And there is another important connection with Kabbalistic tradition. In Lurianic thought, the vessels of Creation break because what God has to say, His name, is too strong for His words; in "Organic Bloom," the brain bursts because, like the vessels of Creation, it is unable to contain its own thinking processes. Which brings me to my third point. "Organic Bloom" pictures the mind continually evading and escaping itself, paradoxically extending beyond its own contours. While in this early poem, the mind's expansiveness takes a Freudian form, with forgotten — or repressed — guilt and sin relegated to regions of mind still uncharted, nearly fifty years later, Kunitz's fascination with inclusiveness turns up again, this time stripped of all psychoanalytic thinking. In a conversation with Christopher Busa, originally taped in 1977, and now printed in *Next-To-Last-Things*, Kunitz says: "I sometimes think I ought to spend the rest of my life writing a single poem whose action reaches an epiphany only at the point of exhaustion, in the combustion of the whole life, and continues and renews, until it blows away like a puff of milkweed." When I read this passage, I immediately thought of "Organic Bloom." As in that early poem, the thinking process, for Kunitz, is still organic, its rhythms comparable to the cycles of plant life. There is even the same combustive energy, the thinking process exploding, blowing away like a puff of milkweed. And finally, there is the same desire for inclusiveness, a need to record the mental processes of a lifetime in a single poem. Kunitz himself has observed: "Occasionally, I am astonished to find, through all the devious windings of a poem, that my destination is something I've written months or years before, embedded in a notebook or recorded on a crumpled scrap of paper, perhaps the back of an envelope. That is what the poem, in its blind intuitive way, has been seeking out. The mind's stuff is wonderfully patient" (*A Kind of Order, A Kind of Folly*).

But while the model Kunitz proposes for a single poem is reminiscent of "Organic Bloom" in some ways, in other respects it is very different. Where the sonnet stressed the compactness of the brain, the more recent model emphasizes the vast realms of space human consciousness contains — and not only because this single poem would follow the action of the whole life. Kunitz has replaced the image of fruit with the image of the milkweed pod. When milkweed explodes, the seed-bearing puffs do not blow away all at once; they lift into the air at rhythmic intervals, blowing away gradually, fitfully. And the journey they trace in the air includes not only the puffballs, but the spaces between their eruptions: just as in passages of music where there are many rests, the pauses are meant to be heard and the listener must feel the musicians playing the silences as well as the notes. When, in his conversation with Busa, Kunitz talks of organizing his poems spatially — "I follow the track of the eye — it's a track through space" — I see those puffs of milkweed, the intervals between them. Poets' models, the blueprints or maps for poems they hope to write, are peculiar because they tend to combine qualities that are essentially incompatible. In a poem that has always impressed me as Elizabeth Bishop's own aesthetic model, she describes a monument that would certainly never stand, but that brings together through its architectural peculiarities contradictory elements in her own style, which combines the exotic with the domestic, the highly ornate with the plain:

Then on the topmost cube is set
a sort of fleur-de-lys of weathered wood,
long petals of board, pierced with odd holes,
four-sided, stiff ecclesiastical.
("The Monument")

And there is a poem by A. R. Ammons, "The Arc Inside and Out," which reconciles in the image of "periphery enclosing our system with its bright dot," Ammons' own opposing needs: the minimalist need for "the impoverished diamond" and the "heap shoveler's" need for sheer "plentitude." Kunitz's model implies a need to give form to consciousness itself — to stand somehow outside the workings of his own mind so that he can discover the shape of what is essentially elusive because it is in a continual state of becoming: or, as Kunitz succinctly stated the paradox in an early poem, "Change" — "Becoming, never being, till / Becoming is a being still." Combustive, agitated, explosive — Kunitz's model is primarily kinesthetic, the whole life danced out, with the image of the milkweed giving visual form to a process that is first felt inside the body as rhythm. "Even before it is ready to change into language," Kunitz says, "a poem may begin to assert its buried life in the mind with wordless surges of rhythm and counter-rhythm. Gradually the rhythms attach themselves to objects and feelings" (*A Kind of Order, A Kind of Folly*). To discover the rhythms by which the mind beats out its thoughts, to find the pattern in what is continually moving, dying and renewing — all this is implied by Kunitz's model for a poem that would record the combustion of the whole life. Unlike other models of artistic inclusiveness — Marcel Duchamp's *Box in a Valise* (1941), for example, which contains miniature reproductions of nearly all his works — Kunitz's model is not stationary, but in motion: it pulses with thought.

As I read Kunitz's *Next-To-Last Things* during my long night of insomnia, it seemed to me that the single poem whose action continues and renews until it blows away like a puff of milkweed was quite possibly this book. For one thing, *Next-To-Last Things* has "world enough, and time" to be that poem, more world and time than any of Kunitz's previous books.

Though its first section is made up of only thirteen poems, that section alone enacts a drama that moves simultaneously through three different levels of time — personal, mythical, and creative. With the first poem, "The Snakes of

September," the speaker is in a garden that could be Kunitz's own garden at 32 Commercial Street, but we are also reminded of that other mythical Garden by two snakes entwined "in a brazen loveknot," as if defiant of the Fall. With the last poem, "The Wellfleet Whale," there is again a personal experience drawn from Kunitz's own life, his encounter with a finback whale, foundered and dying on Wellfleet beach, an encounter which appears to be a manifestation of a greater mythical event. Because many phrases in the poem — phrases like "news of your advent," "keepers of the nightfall watch," "hour of desolation," and "huge lingering passion" — allude to Christ's Passion and because the tourists and souvenir-hunters who crowd around the whale, carving initials in its flanks and peeling strips of its skin, recall the crowds of Christ's tormentors depicted in the great Renaissance paintings by Bruegel and Bosch, this poem, like the first in this section, enacts a mythical, as well as a personal drama: a drama that takes in the grand sweep of Christian time from the Creation to the Passion — and also redefines one aspect of that drama, the Fall. For Kunitz, the Fall does not seem to be caused either by human pride or human yearning for more knowledge (Kunitz is too fearless a transgressor of limits to accept such interpretations). Rather, the Fall is displaced from the Garden, which remains defiantly innocent, to the scene of Christ's death on the cross; i.e., the Fall coincides with the loss of our greatest human ideals, with the loss of those figures that, like the whale — "pure energy incarnate / as nobility of form" — embody beauty, majesty, grace, with the loss of those ideal forms that thrill us, stirring our wonder and awe. When the speaker of "The Wellfleet Whale" expresses his sense of loss — "You have become like us, / disgraced and mortal" — I feel as if a curtain had suddenly been ripped, as if the very fabric of life has been torn. Whatever the reader is going to do with this profoundly disturbing revelation will require time, and therefore, the book wisely provides no more poems. Instead of comfort, it offers

18

the reader another mode of thinking entirely: the second half of the book consists of a rich variety of prose genres — essay, memoir, conversation, and journal entry — all sustaining a kind of fugal dialogue with one another, as well as with the poems in the opening section. While several memoirs extend the poet's personal history with rich remembrances of close friends, the poet Robert Lowell and the artist Philip Guston, and even take the reader back to Kunitz's childhood with the story of his mother, Yetta Helen Dine, the major thrust of the prose, it seems to me, is toward an exploration of the creative process, as particularized in Kunitz's own experiences. Not only do several of the essays explore the origins of some of Kunitz's poems, but through the inclusion of so many different prose forms, this section seems to embody the creative impetus of the thinking process itself, as mind continually finds new shapes to renew itself. From the more intuitive thinking of the earlier poems, this section shifts to the more cognitive, more rational thinking of the essay. From the more extroverted thinking of conversation and interview, to the more introspective thinking of the journal. These forms of thinking even vary as to how much silence — or space — they include, with the more fragmented journal entries awash in silence, a veritable archipelago of thoughts where mind trails off into the wild waters just beyond the limits of rational thinking, into what Kunitz might call "clouds of our unknowing." As in this journal entry: "When the Tzartkover Rabbi, celebrated in Hasidic lore, was asked his reason for failing to preach Torah for a long time, he gave his answer: 'There are seventy ways of reciting Torah. One of them is through silence.'" By contrast, the conversation with Busa, which incidentally provides the best interview of Kunitz that I know of, is tightly packed, the voices of poet and interviewer spiraling around one another, braiding into intricate patterns of thought which suddenly unravel into a new design.

Because the book's second section not only explores the creative process as a discussible subject, but also embodies that process through its own shape-shifting, certain poems in the first section, which themselves are concerned with poetic composition, are suddenly reactivated by the prose pieces. The reader goes back to "The Round," a poem which dramatizes through its own circular structure the poet's cyclic activity, his daily round, with its deep immersion in writing: as the poem closes, the speaker is scribbling on the blotted page the very words that began the poem — "Light splashed . . ." What Kunitz envisioned in an early poem — "The end and the beginning in each other's arms" ("Open The Gates") — is not fulfilled through the form of "The Round" which, like the mythical uroborus, that circular snake which grasps its own tail in its mouth, wraps around itself. "The Wellfleet Whale" provides another look at the creative process. The poem begins with a journal entry, not a simulated journal entry, but a real excerpt which can be found in an earlier collection of Kunitz's prose pieces, *A Kind of Order, A Kind of Folly*. Beginning with the journal account allows Kunitz to overcome certain technical problems: for example, it frees him to plunge immediately into a lyrical address to the whale because he can count on the journal notation to ground the reader in all the necessary narrative information. But the journal-entry beginning also accomplishes something else. It allows the reader to discover those places where the poem has changed and transformed the original anecdote. As the reader compares the journal's account of Kunitz's encounter with the whale with the poem's account, reading recreates the process of poetic composition, that wonderful period of indeterminancy where even the poem's structure is in a state of flux. To discover that the poem has substituted a we for the first person singular point of view of the journal is to reach that place in the creative process where a decision was made, where the possibility of a crowd scene suggestive of the crowds that milled around the dying Christ, may first have occurred to the poet. Where the journal entry is anecdotal, verging on insight, the poem is interpretative — the world it presents charged with meaning.

I suspect that it is the way in which the second section of *Next-To-Last Things* returns us to the poems of the first section, inviting us to read those poems through its own interest in the creative process, that finally provides the comfort which "The Wellfleet Whale" at first denies. As Yeats wisely understood, "All things fall and are built again, And those that build them again are gay." The second section invites us to enter into the history of the poems in the first section, to explore the layers of experience they shape and transform: to reread "The Abduction," this time knowing something about its origins in Kunitz's reading on UFO adventures; to return even to a poem from an earlier book, "Green Ways," this time with the knowledge of Keats's influence on Kunitz's imagination. To read the poems in this way is to unsettle them, to return them to that place of pure becoming, that "terrible threshold" where the poet hears "a rush of forms" ("Open The Gates"). *Next-To-Last Things* is more filled with process, with the action of the mind, with poems caught in the act of becoming than any other Kunitz book, which is my other reason for thinking that this book is the combustion of a whole life. Most poets feel regret over what gets left out of their poems, and Kunitz, I think, is no exception. "Language overwhelms the poet in a shapeless rush," he writes. "It's a montage, an overlapping of imagery, feelings, thoughts, sounds, sensations, which have not yet submitted to regimentation" (*A Kind of Order, A Kind of Folly*). The shapeless rush has energy, excitement, vigor: the mouth filled with the poem in all its rich simultaneity, none of the wild feathers plucked. Some of the greatest poets have tried to preserve in their poems the shifting shapes of pure becoming when the poem dazzles with kaleidoscopic possibilities. Chaucer's dream-poems, for example, appear to simulate early, rougher stages of their own composition, thus recording, or seeming to record, a series of broken-off attempts: they grow around these earlier versions the way a tree grows around its own rings. But it was especially Dante who sought to preserve the emotional state that accompanied the writing of those poems addressed to Beatrice. That strange book, the *Vita Nuova*, alternates between sections of poetry and sections of prose, with the prose sections describing the circumstances of poetic composition. Since these circumstances often place a feverish, love-sick Dante at celebrations, banquets, and funerals where he is surrounded by shifting crowds of young women, Beatrice's friends, finally, those crowds which keep reforming, flowing into new shapes, become a metaphor for Dante's state of creative flux and seem as much a part of the poet's visionary experience, his own teeming mind, as a part of his daily, quotidian experience. So imperceptibly do vision and reality shade into one another in the *Vita Nuova* that at times it is impossible to tell them apart. Dante keeps the reader positioned at that edge where the creative impulse keeps surging up, an edge so fine it is like an imaginary number, the square root of minus one, that symbol i which Leibniz called "an amphibian between being and nonbeing."

Perhaps it was my reading the *Vita Nuova* during the same night that I read Kunitz's book that made me especially sensitive to what I had missed on previous readings: the way so many of the poems in *Next-To-Last Things* seem to catch the very moment when they were first heard or glimpsed or sensed. The poems straddle that edge where the non-verbal rush of forms is first translated into words. Listen to the beginnings of two of the poems, "The Snakes of September,"

All summer I heard them
rustling in the shrubbery,
outracing me from tier
to tier in my garden,
a whisper among the viburnums,
a signal flashed from the hedgerow,
a shadow pulsing

in the barberry thicket

and now "The Image-Maker,"

A wind passed over my mind,
insidious and cold.
It is a thought, I thought,
but it was only its shadow.
Words came,
or the breath of my sisters,
with a black rustle of wings.

The poems begin at the threshold of perception where seeing
and hearing scorn the sense organs. Such poems upset the read-
er's orientation, for there is always more *out there*, they suggest,
than the reader at first supposed. To a great extent, it is the
forms and shapes that keep looking in at the poems' speakers,
like the "heavy furpiece" pressed to the screen door in
"Raccoon Journal" and "the bleached faces peering in / with
coals for eyes" in "The Abduction," that make the reader so
keenly aware of realms of space that keep growing vast and
vaster, realms that elude human knowledge. But another, per-
haps more important factor, is the way the poems' speakers
keep pressing for a knowledge of their world that continually
escapes them:

Some things I do not profess
To understand, perhaps
not wanting to, including
whatever it was they did
with you or you with them
that timeless summer day
when you stumbled out of the wood,
distracted, with your white blouse torn
and a bloodstain on your skirt.

The woman described in the opening lines of "The Abduction" now lies beside the poem's speaker, as mysterious, as unknowable as the UFOs that perhaps abducted her into outer space — of the men, "a dumbshow retinue / in leather shrouds" who, more probably, gang-raped her. All the speaker has to offer the reader — and himself — are what the woman he loves has pieced together with him over the years; that is to say, what he has to offer are interpretations of an event that may itself be a fiction. "What do we know," the speaker concludes, "beyond the rapture and the dread?" What do we know, in other words, beyond the emotions stirred up by our own versions of the world, our own myths? With the concluding question, inner space becomes as vast and unknowable as outer space. And like the man depicted in "The Long Boat," whose "boat has snapped loose / from its moorings," the reader is also set adrift, "rocked by the Infinite!"

When I started to read *Next-To-Last Things*, I had expected to hear a voice I already knew, the generic Kunitz made familiar by all the particular encounters I have had with him — as his student at Columbia University, as a fellow at the Fine Arts Work Center, as audience at many of his poetry readings. Instead, I heard someone or something else, a thrilling presence, disembodied as the birdsong that kept erupting into my long night of insomnia. In a fascinating exchange that is preserved in Busa's interview of Kunitz, poet and interviewer distinguish between "the varied voice of personality, the voice that speaks in the context of a dramatic situation," and the voice of incantation, made up of sound and rhythm. The voice I heard that night was neither the voice of personality nor the incantatory voice, but a more impersonal, universal presence that seemed to sound from the beauty of shapes, from the primordial structures of the thinking process itself. I call this the ecstatic voice, and by ecstatic, I do not mean what I think many people mean when they use that word incorrectly as a synonym for euphoric. I am using ecstatic in its root sense to mean standing outside of or apart from or beyond one's usual self or one's usual sense of the world. The ecstatic voice articulates the shifting shapes of pure becoming, of mind exceeding itself, and is kin to the grand, protean structures of the natural world: those thunderheads that pile up on the horizon during Florida's rainy season, cumulonimbus balanced on cumulonimbus, mountainous altars to abundance, altars so affluent they can afford to spend themselves in further expansions, puffing up into anvil-shaped towers, until suddenly the altar topples, itself the sacrifice, spilling down as rain. While I sensed the ecstatic voice everywhere in *Next-To-Last Things*, I heard it especially in "The Image-Maker," a poem that seems miraculous to me in the way it moves at the very limits of consciousness, and in its closing lines, even extends a little beyond those limits through the sheer efforts of envisioning them:

I listen, but I avert my ears
from Meister Eckhart's warning:
All things must be forsaken.
God Scorns
to show Himself among images.

Though the image-maker averts his ears from the master's warning, the reader of the poem, who now conceives of an imageless form of thinking, who probes its possibility, feels as if some boundary has just been transgressed. Perhaps the poem has led the reader to imagine life after death, a realm of shapes so pure they scorn particulars. Wherever the reader had been led, it is not a place visited before. The brain has just advanced into its own uncharted territory, paradoxically exceeding its own limits.

Susan Mitchell

LOST PARROT

She can cry his name from today to tomorrow.
She can Charlie him this, cracker him that, there
in the topmost he hangs like
a Christmas ornament,
his tail
a cascade of emeralds and limes.

The child is heartsick. She has taped messages
to the mailboxes, the names
he responds to, his favorite seeds.
At twilight she calls and calls.

Oh, Charlie, you went everywhere with her,
to the post office and the mall, to the women's
room at the Marriott where you perched
on the stall, good-natured, patient.

And didn't you love to take her thumb
in your golden beak
and, squeezing tenderly, shriek and shriek
as if your own gentleness
were killing you?

You were her darling, her cinnamon stick, her pedagogue.
You knew her secret names
in Persian and ancient Greek. At the beach
you had your own chair and umbrella.
Oh, pampered bird. The neighbors sympathize. But what's
love compared with wild red fruit, a big
gold moon, and an evening that smells of paradise?

If she were older, she'd join the other
sad girls for drinks, she'd lick
the salt from her tequila glass and say something wise
she'd heard said a hundred times before.
Love is a cage she's glad to be free of.

Oh, Charlie, you were her pope and popinjay,
her gaudy, her flambeau, her magnificat.
You were the postcard
each morning delivered to her room, her all-day sunset.

In the topmost fronds you squall and squawk
to the other flashy runaways,
Say paradise! No dice, no dice.

Robert Bly

WITH LOVE FOR STANLEY

Well, there is something fierce looking out from behind this perturbable face of words there is someone fierce as the black-funneled twister that dismantled the house in the sugar maples. Already as a boy he was wily and fierce enough to enjoy Frieda, and so testify that he was the son of his father, just as Lincoln was, "tall and lonely". It does no good to defeat a fierce man like this; he'll reappear twenty years later as a knot still glowing in the lintel, and he is willing to demand that his father bless his good right arm.

This fierceness is not a boy's energy; it is a man blinded with Dante's key. He is a salmon packed with dozens of sharp bones — "limber and firm in the state of his shining" — sharp enough so that he is an 'I' with fins. He didn't choose the way; "the way chose me." *Come. Bathe in these waters. Increase and die.* That is a lively challenge he has left behind for the younger poets. The fierce man looking out from his mask of water says, Go ahead: "Inherit my salt kingdom." I dare you. A good challenge from the salt-father.

Seamus Heaney

THE BOILING HOUSE

Four doors: calves' house, the middle house, the boiling house, the home house. In census terms, three outbuildings, one dwelling. All under the one run of thatched roof, behind one whitewashed, single-storeyed wall.

The boiling house too had been a dwelling once. Now it was dug-out dark, peat-dry and oddly sound-proofed, a storage place for bags of meal and grain. But in the meantime it had lived the scullion life that seethed still in its name.

Heating of gruel, boiling of brock, slop-renderings, washes, fowl-feeds, pig-swill, hot water for pig-killings, for scouring of churns and pails, for extra pots on the crane at harvest homes.

At the moment of a death (Romans believed) the soul resolved into three. The *manes* went to Elysian fields or deeper, to Tartarus. The *anima* returned itself to the gods; and the *umbra* hovered, unwilling to quit the body.

I am content with that, and opt for a hover-home where others hovered. An old reluctant breath comes off the bags. A pelt of soot is trembling in the chimney. The clay floor has stayed obstinate and simple.

W.S. Merwin

April 18, 2001

Dear Stanley,

　　Poems of yours which I know by heart are all around me, and tapes of your readings accompany me in the car. The garden reminds me of your so different garden on a different coast. You are more often in my mind than you would believe, and that is true of so many of us.

　　How the years pass I cannot, even now, imagine. When it does not seem that they have passed at all. I so wish we could have your July celebration together but I will be thinking of you with fond disbelief — of the numbers, you know, for you, dear friend, are perennial. I send you congratulations, old seasoned gratitude, and great affection, as I hope you know. Love to you and Elise from Paula and me,

William

William

And I hope you like this poem.

W.S. Merwin

TO IMPATENCE

(for Stanley Kunitz)

Don't wish your life away
my mother said and I saw
past her words that same day
suddenly not there
nor the days after
even the ones I remember

and though hands held back the hounds
on the way to the hunt
now the fleet deer are gone
that bounded before them
all too soon overtaken
as she knew they would be

and well as she warned me
always calling me home
to the moment around me
that was taking its good time
and willingly though I
heeded her words to me
once again waking me
to the breath that was there

you too kept whispering
up close to my ear
the secrets of hunger
for some prize not yet there
sight of face touch of skin

light in another valley
labor triumphant or
last word of a story
without which you insisted
the world would not be complete
soon soon you repeated
it cannot be too soon

yet you know it can
and you know it would be
the end of you too only
if ever it arrives
you find something else missing
and I know I must thank you
for your faithful discontent
and what it has led me to
yes yes you have guided me
but what it is hard now to see
is the mortal hurry

Richard Wilbur

Cummington

Dear Stanley,

I ought to have some substantial new poem on hand with
which to celebrate the 96th of Stanley the jack-of-all, who is
not only a peerless poet but also a peerless gardener, a car-
penter, and a cook. If I could hail you in clerihews I would
do so, but I can find no rhymes for Kunitz other than moon
bits and prune pits. I shall have to fall back on a children's
book I'm writing, which is about how some words have
other words inside them. For instance,

In a flower-bed, the rows of bright-faced plants

Look like a choir that's singing hymns and chants

And psalms and Christmas carols. That's how come

We find an <u>anthem</u> in <u>Chrysanthemum</u>.

I know you would never organize a garden in such a stodgy
row-by-row manner, but in any case here are some hymns
and chants and bouquets from

Dick

Tory Dent

WHEN ATHEISTS PRAY

(for Stanley Kunitz)

Who, if I cried, would hear me among the angelic orders?

And how should we know, by what sign, by what feeling,
that they've heard us? We watch the sky darken, a cold heart
at noon regardless of expectation, regardless of desire and its
intensity, not the rioting red of white cell-producing hope,
nor the leech-bled black-purple of bottomlessness. No senti-
ment, no matter how exigently soulful, proves exigent
enough.

First we petition with respectful prayers, careful dance steps,
complete obedience. There follows, after having endured
days of bread and water, impatient prayers, our eyebrows
furrowing, our knees twitching in genuflection. And then
like machine gunfire detected from a distant bunker, crypti-
cally faint and time-delayed in their imploding, our fears
infect us: no prayers will be heard, let alone answered.

*And even if one of them suddenly pressed me against his heart, I
should fade in the strength of his stronger existence;*

For the impressive indifference of angels is greater than our
ungainly desires, until our desires, to the extent they're unat-
tended, redouble in their need, accelerating exponentially
until ultimately they dispel, deflect, Trojan spears off the
shield of Achilles— or pass through, cruelly, without pene-
tration, like breeze through a metal screen or the free world

glimpsed through wrought-iron bars. Our human fists fly wild through ghostly anatomy, through the free world of their love, later realized as false. But the visceral memory, our essential, insistent belief, though erased instantly from consciousness still resonates in our pulse, wish-fragments of sorts, as if dismembered in the cleaving wake of a shooting star.

For Beauty's nothing but beginning of Terror we're still just able to bear, and why we adore it so is because it serenely disdains to destroy us.

Nature was not always a thing of beauty. Once fishermans' houses were built with their backs toward the ocean in an effort to ignore the dreaded, devouring, ionizing body with its braying surf, breached in constant threat, flagellating the bosky shoreline day and night; the Creator represented in briny incarnation, fanged and punishing as the father we later configured in the concept of the super-ego. But no theory can subvert our infantile wishes for love beyond what we've invented; what's humanly contrived will always appear somehow low brow and insufficient, no replacement for the sublime affliction of our origin, no substantial explanation for the breccia-like womb we refer back to, and refer back to . . . Hence the necessity for angels, more crucial than the bread and water we're readily willing to do without for one remarkable acknowledgment from them, one conciliatory response that they care. We return to angels like dog to grave of dead master, out of lack of recourse for something stronger than ourselves, because we cannot make sense of suffering. Because we cannot comprehend, cannot contain within our puny, mortal minds a world like this that allows— no, orchestrates— with almost Caligulean joy, life events to unfold so disproportionately, we assign meaning to the immaterial to supplement our loneliness. Because we cannot make sense of suffering, the gross marginalization of its subjects, we imagine the world as beautiful in order to counteract, even transform, the depravity inside us, despite the masochistic agenda we know by now to be the outcome— because too unbearable, too unrecognizable is the thought that we're just set loose amidst this brazen arbitrariness, too anachronistically barbaric the isolation of pain without reason, pain without rescue, without consolation, without medicine.

Therefore, years may pass before we've stopped rationalizing that perhaps the angels are hard of hearing, that it's the effort to listen, to turn their dear, deaf cherubic ears closer, which instigates even the smallest birds, especially the ones known for love-calls so melodic they play in the carbon monoxide increasing air like harpsichord music, to fall in fists of dirt, like rain that tears into flesh; to fall as if thrown out of oblivion into oblivion, massacred bodies into mass graves, the skulls of children split apart for the fun of it.

Each single angel is terrible.

But we continue living, continue eating, continue fucking, praying to the fantasy of mercy. Until we recognize, as if shaken, the intolerable for what it truly is, our adaptable, pathetic souls, malleable as Playskool putty, having internalized so successfully the slavemaster within us, any autonomous action expunged long ago from the pretence of possibility; until degenerating in the poverty of the self-mortification of our believing, we finally perceive how pitiful an act the behavior of praying be; it be the act of begging, really . . .

And so I keep down my heart and swallow the call-note of depth-dark sobbing.

36

What's most terrifying resounds as wings, swooping closer—
the angels that operate as passive spectators while heinous
things take place. And if prayers ever do reveal themselves as
if answered, it's so late that it's the stumps of our amputated
limbs we thank them for, so desecrated by loss and disease
are we by then, our most natural, instinctual capacity to love
ruined, pitted, abolished.

Hence, I refuse to look upward, upward to a canopy of pre-
supposed atonement. What were once prayers for readiness
to reckon with disappointment become angry, incriminating
prayers, prayers of ultimatum— until those prayers, those
useless elocutions from our humiliated hearts, evolve into, or
rather grow up into, articulations of atheism, pronounce-
ments of love retracted, of love regretfully spent. We express
instead, spitting out and upward, hoping to reach the hem-
lines of their robes, war-waging rage on our enemy angels
who obviously prolong our torment and revel in it; angels
whose profiles must have pivoted away from us at birth, self-
preoccupied as aristocrats, demonstrating the vanity of
angels, their deficit of compassion. We despise their selfish
motives, the insensitive personalities of angels. O fascist
angel, I visualize your death, angelless, alone in the hospital,
powers foreclosed in the last stages of cancer or AIDS. I will
the nurse who's responsible for your pain medication to run
behind schedule and be unable to be located, so that you die,
horrid angel, a horrible death; so that you die incrementally,
without honor or counsel, while I get to watch, like a vic-
tim's family member in the auditorium of your execution
chamber. I regard you coldly as if I were an angel, while you
pray to angels, pray to me. I observe disdainfully while you
pray hard for pardon, matted wings shaking with emphasis,
your idiot angel eyes clouding up, cataracts incurred by grief.
You pray, which means you beg from me, homeless angel,

veteran angel, criminal angel, for the pain to stop. But the pain will not stop; it will not, my angel. I shake my head, shrug. "But these are the mysteries of life," I say with my shoulders, my pretend wings. I enjoy your suffering as you enjoyed mine. I remain mute as you cry out to me, smile down on your grimaced face, your tiny angel tears minute as glass shards from where I view you, avenged behind the dou-ble-glass window. Sweet syringe of your lethal injection, let no execution be too quick for you, too humane, too angel-like in leniency.

Alas, who is there we can make use of? Not angels, not men;

For when I first found out I was HIV positive on April 12, 1988, over a payphone at an artist colony in upstate New York, in a windowless, wainscoted phone closet, a single bare bulb suspended above me like the enucleated eye of some god surveying its work, enshrouding me in its newfound blindness. My death began there like a crash test for my death, the plastic skin and synthetic brain of my anthropo-morphic body, wired to measure pain, but feeling nothing. My death began there with the crisis of stigma, the social death which precludes the physical death of AIDS and is the essence of discrimination. My death began there, my fears instantaneously transposed upon the cute, bucolic landscape, the mise-en-scene of their materialization too demonically devised, too identical to science fiction to assimilate. But they happened all right, unfolding, perverse canon of events, exactly as I imagined in my worst case scenarios. Each level of the disease, the gradations of physical recession, the lungs, the gut, the eyes, the brain— systems of torture, instigated by an interrogator I cannot target beyond the decoy glare of the bare bulb, that enucleated eye of some god with a flair for persecution. No lull, no pause, no relief, no differentia-tion befell the blank predatory moments of anticipation that

seized me upon waking— slow-acting, time-released seizures
of terror— stretched out on a rack over the course of thir-
teen years (and it's not over yet)—

My death began there with my social death, wood cross
burning on front lawn. My death began there while, as if
bound up and gagged, I was ordered to look at my own
death rehearsed in the death of friends and neighbors and
fellow patients. My home, my life metamorphosed into a
caricature or pastiche of itself, dwarfed amid the larger-than-
life plague I embodied. Furniture shrank, voices dimmed and
echoed as if upon a stage set whose props, their solitariness
offset by the defamiliarization of their context, posited them-
selves as surreal emblems of the way my life had broken
off— not organically like a lightning-struck branch churning
swiftly along river rapids, but intentionally, serially, a decap-
itated head symbolic of more than just mine, knocking in
thuds and blood spurts down to a blackened, ostracized
earth. My death began there, drawn out sadistically by the
human phenomenon of waiting within the re-creation of
that phone booth, which transfigured every room thereafter
into a solitary, windowless, wainscoted cell. I waited for my
life to revert back, suddenly, same as it had split off, sutured
together without noticeable scar. I waited for my life to
return to me, as if MIA while I whispered lamentations at an
inert photograph.

   . . . and already the knowing brutes are aware that we don't
feel very securely at home within our interpreted world.

I waited nowhere, while I groped from room to room,
through the solitary routine of rising out of bed, getting
through the day, putting myself back to bed. I relied primari-
ly on sound, smell and touch: alarming clock and Pledge
scented desk, dish-crammed sink, hot cup, ringing phone,

breaking bus, wind racked tree, loud conversation in which I'm oddly a participant with friend, nurse, doctor, insurance representative— each and all banal and aloof, ineffectual to stop my death, social and physical, from coming apocalyptically upon me. In alternate shifts, skin-burning daylight and skin-burning moonlight inconsequentially shined above daily evidence of the dead and almost dead, as if a successful plan for extermination were taking place (the act of inaction no less culpable and you know exactly what I'm talking about). I waited for my death to finish itself, to complete its trajectory from fetus to ash, to halt in the gristly air of absolute end, for my body to collapse, exhausted animal beneath me. I waited hospitalized, or at home on IV, hair falling out, drugged 'til comatose, drugged 'til poisoned, my body turning in against itself in the breakdown of its civil discontent. As if undergoing shock treatment, I convulsed and winced submerged amidst, within, that evidence of the dead and almost dead, the atmosphere of stark *au revoir*, the non-stop wrench of separation, not entirely unlike those waving children and screaming parents during the Kindertransport exodus in Poland.

So when I say I believe in nothing, I mean just that. To the leaves gone brown and dry, to winter land, its vengeful groundswells and black ice, I direct my anti-prayers, desperate exhalations, that's all. Bitter condemnations heard by no one, absorbed by nothing, mere brow-furrowing, wet lips frozen in their tremble. My beliefs, blood-sucking shadows, perpetuate themselves paradoxically by virtue of their nihilism, the way a respirator provides the semblance of life. The evidence of nothingness, upon which my beliefs feed, proliferates, regretfully fecund and lush in what should be a generic finisterre. They make a mockery of the bygone lovechild, hopeful once, its lit wick of unconscious desire despite cranial damage. The brain-death of conscious want has already been pronounced, but still the infantile reflex of working mouth sucks from invisible nipple as it does artifical air from plastic tube, until a judge decides otherwise.

There remains, perhaps, some tree on a slope, to be looked at day after day, there remains for us yesterday's walk and the cupboard-love loyalty of a habit that liked us and stayed and never gave notice.

There remains now, thirteen years later, only the orator of angels. Only the author of angelic disappointment could make me raise my face, queerly optimistic again, although underneath it like honey comb within hive, catacombs of grief lie dug twelve feet deep— Only momentarily quiescent do they reside beneath that ingenuous, rose-petal self-portrait I stare at, estranged, from somewhere else,

Oh, and there's Night there's Night, when the wind full of cosmic space feeds on our faces: for whom would she not remain, longer for, mild disenchantress, painfully there for the lonely heart to achieve?

Why did I choose Rilke's first elegy as my wedding day vow? Because only concurrent with an affirmation of godlessness could I make such a promise, could my vows be held accountable; in no other eyes but mine, peering down, beady iron of gargoyle or prismatic orb of angel, upon my reciting tongue— O heart exposed to the rudimentary decisions of survival, crude and emotion defying; to the self-scrutiny of defining integrity within that survival, which is its only means of definition, which is the only means of survival. My heart I would judge and judge harshly. Only in this chapel, the most spare space as testimony to the impermanence of lonely dogwood, distant city, frail wedding bouquet, beloved metaphors for an anemic future which no one escapes—

would loyalty form; where the death-laugh, the death-cry, of
my near death, procures and confirms the certainty of
insignificance— afternoon moor mist nullified by lucky
moonlessness.

*Is she lighter for lovers? Alas, with each other they only conceal
their lot!*

No night was not lighter for us, mentor poet, especially on
that night when Sean and I prayed, under a matte black sky
wherein all stars had previously been deported and ghet-
toized. Only the moon, like a penitentiary yard search-and-
surveillance light, strobed past our petitioning hands, me in
bed as Sean knelt against it, elbows leaning into my hipline.
I had requested this as a last resort. So we prayed, atheists
both of us, despite ourselves, in conflict with ourselves—who
we knew ourselves to be versus whom we were forced to
become. We hated the world that forced us to do so, the
calamity of angels which defaced us gleefully in their light;
belittled us beneath the vile featheriness of their interwoven
wings; their pinched judgmental expressions, their pursed
lips, rasping *tsk-tsks* like the rattle of hunger from viper
snakes. We no longer negotiated, we no longer promised, we
did not implore or urge or plead, appeal, blandish, woo,
worship or canvass. We begged. We begged, and although
together, we begged alone (for a beggar is always unto him-
self, alone in the humiliation of begging), mouths disfigured
by the unfamiliar intention, our self-betrayal like the self-
inflicted wounds with which beggars in Calcutta eagerly
maim themselves in order to become better beggars. We
begged from the white of the moon's eye for my eyesight,
begged from electrically heated air for our life together. We
begged from the ceiling plaster, from the Venetian blinds,
from the New York skyline. We begged from traffic, from
sirens, from doormen, garbage chutes, pharmacists, and
Chinese food delivery boys.

This is what suffering reduces you to. As the Hanoi Hilton inmates can attest, those who signed confessions after weeks, months, years of extensive torture—"they *can* make you do what you don't want to do." So we begged from North Vietnamese angels; Nazi party angels; African Apartheid angels; Reagan Conservative angels; yoked and harnessed by their self-imposed mythological glory, their smug, omniscient unattainableness. And we actually cried from the inanition of our begging, so very attainable were we in contrast. Our words uttered in unison, words gestated in the stomach and groin rather than larynx, brought us as if strong-arming us to tears, to cry the spirit-breaking kind of cry only total defeat produces— the self-lacerating, wholly humiliating, soul-eradicating kind; the wounded, the tortured, the sick, the lynched, the historically persecuted kind; the kind emitted perhaps from those engraved names we read non-sensically after a while, like calligraphy or hieroglyphs, on memorial monuments decades later: those multitudinous objects of genocide who most likely begged, in rushed elliptical entreaties, for their life from the small, dark corner of what's left of their life.

Don't you know yet?—

You, who have not had to beg yet, listen to the coffin maker running out of nails. Listen to the yelling of babies, orphaned and red-cell depleted who must receive transfusions with HIV-contaminated blood because the clinics can't afford the requisite lab equipment for seropositve testing. There are no metaphors, no "happening" adjectives, or interesting, original uses of language, no new line breaks. You just have to smell it— the dense smoke from the bonfire of mass cremations. It's not the aroma of a Diptych candle to which you're accustomed, now is it?

Fling the emptiness out of your arms into the space we breathe—

Surrender to the common puddle right in front of you, for therein harbors, in your fun house reflection, the possibility that by drowning you may die.

Surrender to "the luxury of a boring evening," as one Holocaust survivor put it.

Surrender to the compulsion to move forward, to silly expectancy, to your evaluation of life, not regardless of, but precisely because of, all the arbitrary clear-cutting of precious growth you've beheld. Surrender within, despite, and in protest to the thick, non-retractable memory of begging. Avenge the angels, and surrender to that instinctual capacity to love which they've worked so hard to destroy, conceding to what you don't want to admit, for not only angels have failed you.

maybe that the birds will feel the extended air in more intimate flight.

— those birds, the few left in the disinfected sky, the survivors of angels; the crow caws we hear in lieu of harpsichord music, strangely sustaining us.

Rainer Maria Rilke's First Duino Elegy
translated by J. B. Leishman and Stephen Spender

Yusef Komunyakaa

BLESSING THE ANIMALS

Two by two, past
the portals of paradise,
camels & pythons parade.
As if on best behavior,
civil as robed billy goats
& Big Bird, they stroll
down aisles of polished stone
at the Feast of St. Francis.
An elephant daydreams, nudging
ancestral bones down a rocky path,
but won't venture near the boy
with a white mouse peeking
from his coat pocket. Beyond
monkeyshine, their bellows
& cries are like prayers
to unknown planets & zodiac
signs. The ferret & mongoose
on leashes, move as if they know
things with a sixth sense.
Priests twirl hoops of myrrh.
An Australian blue cattle dog
paces a heaven of memories—
a butterfly on a horse's ear
bright as a poppy outside
Urbino. As if crouched
between good & bad, St. John
the Divine grows in quintessence
& limestone, & a hoorah of Miltonic
light falls upon alley rats

awaiting nighttime. Brother
ass, brother sparrowhawk,
& brother dragon. Two
by two, washed & brushed down
by love & human pride,
these beasts of burden
know they're the first
scapegoats. After sacred
oils & holy water, we huddle
this side of their knowing
glances, & they pass through
our lives, still loyal to thorns.

Yusef Komunyakaa

PROVIDENCE

I walked away with your face
stolen from a crowded room,
& the sting of requited memory
lived beneath my skin. A name
raw on my tongue, in my brain, a glimpse
nestled years later like a red bird
among wet leaves on a dull day.

A face. The tilt of a head. Dark
lipstick. *Aletheia.* The unknown
marked on a shoulder, night
weather on our heads.
I pushed out of this half-stunned
yes, begging light, beyond the caul's
shadow, dangling the lifeline of Oh.

I took seven roads to get here
& almost died three times.
How many near misses before
new days slouched into the left corner
pocket, before the hanging fruit
made me kneel? I crossed
five times in the blood to see

the plots against the future—
descendent of a house that knows
all my strong & weak points.
No bounty of love apples glistened
with sweat, a pear-shaped lute

plucked in the valley of the tuber rose
& Madonna lily. Your name untied

every knot in my body, a honey-eating
animal reflected in shop windows
& twinned against this underworld.
Out of tide-lull & upwash
a perfect hunger slipped in
tooled by an eye, & this morning
makes us the oldest song in any god's throat.

We had gone back walking
on our hands. Opened by a kiss,
by fingertips on the Abyssinian
stem & nape, we bloomed
from underneath stone. Moon-pulled
fish skirted the gang-plank,
a dung-scented ark of gopherwood.

Now, you are on my skin, in my mouth
& hair as if you were always
woven in my walk, a rib
unearthed like a necklace of sand dollars
out of black hush. You are a call
& response going back to the first
praise-lament, the old wish

made flesh. The two of us
a third voice, an incantation
sweet-talked & grunted out of The Hawk's
midnight horn. I have you inside
a hard question, & it won't let go,
hooked through the gills & strung up
to the western horizon. We are one,

burning with belief till the thing
inside the cage whimpers
& everything crazes out to a flash
of silver. Begged into the fat juice
of promises, our embrace is a naked
wing lifting us into premonition
worked down to a sigh & plea.

Yusef Komunyakaa

THE SONG THIEF

Up there
in that diorama of morning
light through springtime branches,
how many feathered lifetimes
sifted down through green
leaves, how many wars sprung up
& ended before the cowbird figured out
laws of gravity in Cloudcuckooland,
before the songbird's egg
was nudged from its nest?
Maybe a flock followed a herd
of heifers across a pasture,
pecking wildflower seed
from fresh dung
when the first urge of switcheroo
flashed in their dirt-colored heads.
What nature of creature comforts
taught the unsung cells this art,
this shell game of odds
& percentages in the serpent's leafy
Babylon? Only the cowbird's mating song
fills the air until their young
are ravenous as five
of the seven deadly sins
woven into one.

Maxine Kumin

FOR STANLEY, SOME LINES AT RANDOM

You, Sir, with the red snippers,
who twice saw Halley's comet fly,
you, who can identify
coprinus, chanterelle and sundry
others of the damp-woods fleet,
whose broadside "The Long Boat"
produced on hand-made paper
woven from your discards—
here, the delivery boy declared
is Mr. Kunitz's laundry—
hangs in my study,

it's thirty years since I, a guest
in your Provincetown retreat,
arose from what you said had once been e. e. cummings's bed
to breakfast on an omelet
fat with choice boletuses
that had erupted in your three-tiered garden,
perhaps under one of your dahlias
the size of a dinner plate,
a garden that took decades to create.

Since 1961 we've leaned
against each other, spine
on spine, the luck of the alphabet
to be positioned thus.
Upright or slant, long may we stand
on shelves dusted or not
to be taken up by hands
that cherish us.

Louise Glück

FOUR DREAMS CONCERNING THE MASTER

1. The Supplicant

S. is standing in a small room, reading to himself.
It is a privilege to see S.
alone, in this serene environment.
Only his hand moves, thoughtfully turning the pages.
Then, from under the closed door, a single hazelnut
rolls into the room, coming to rest, at length,
at S.'s foot. With a sigh, S. closes the heavy volume
and stares down wearily at the round nut. "Well," he says,
"what do you want now, Stevens?"

2. Conversation with M.

"Have you ever noticed," he remarked,
"that when women sleep
they're really looking at you?"

3. Noah's Dream

Where were you in the dream?
        The North Pole.

Were you alone?
        No. My friend was with me.

Which friend was that?
>My old friend. My friend the poet.

What were you doing?
>We were crossing a river. But the clumps of ice
>were far apart, we had to jump.

Were you afraid?
>Just cold. Our eyes filled up with snow.

And did you get across?
>It took a long time. Then we got across.

What did you do then, on the other side?
>We walked a long time.

And was the walk the end?
>No. The end was the morning.

4. Conversation with X.

"You," he said, "you're just like Eliot.
You think you know everything in the world
but you don't believe anything."

Kenneth Koch

FOR STANLEY

Stanley, how poets do carry on!
So peculiarly attentive to everything that happens.
Without this, I'd never know, for example,
About your being pickpocketed on a tram
In Rome and your being so angry and then finally so pleased with
                 what you were feeling.
Nor about your secret love, on a campus, nor the mystery of your
                 father,
His inconsiderate disappearance before you were born,
Nor about your encounters with whales and animals and
Insects— "Welcome, eccentric life!" you said to them.
But why do I want to know these things?
The truth is I don't know why, but now that I know them
I know them, you don't have the power to take them back—
And since they have music
Here they are again and again. Thank you for transferring
Them so masterfully, dear friend, from your life to mine!

Carolyn Kizer

THE ANIMAL MASTER

(for Stanley)

When you go for a stroll all kinds of wildlife
creep out from the trees to join you.
Some with a hop or leap
bound to your side. Creatures untamable
seem to salaam or speak to you
as you pass by with your animal followers.

At your house a few enter at once, others pause
on the porch, or lurk by your tidy hedges.
They shadow the walls of your dwelling.
Their hungy chins rest on the windowsills.
Scratching at screens, the timid grow bolder
and sue for permission to enter.

We are let in at once
to crouch near the warmth of your fire.
Noses twitch at delectable odors
that waft from your kitchen,
for you are a master chef as well,
And all will be fed and watered.

When you retire we all want to sleep at your feet,
but there is little unseemly wrestling and shoving.
Some curl up peaceably on the scatter rugs,
on your writing desk, on the laundry hamper.
The rest settle down by the ebbing fire.
We dream manna dreams and honey stanzas.

We wake at a wave of your hand. We are friends
who prance our gratitude, wave clumsy paws,
who hoot, bleat, honk, whinny or neigh,
each having learned to sing his particular song,
all part of the common anthem of creatures.
Now we join to bless and praise our animal master.

Sharon Olds

MEDITATION ON "THE PORTRAIT"

Poems lead mysterious lives. It's a wonder to think of Stanley's poems — some written and perhaps never read, still leading their lives in the bosom of a notebook, like someone who never ventures out of the house into the village, but what travellers most of them have been, voyaging out in breast pockets, and folded up very small in wallets, journeying in books and backpacks, on subways and planes and ocean liners and landing craft, hospitals, prisons, schools, and homes — taped on refrigerators, lying on bedside tables beside the lovers, and beside the solitary sleepers. His poems live in our dreams, in many languages, in many revelations and prayers and turning points and conversations. I recall one evening, sitting late over the dessert and the wine, mulling with dear friends over the slap in "The Portrait," the moment where the widow strikes her son as he's holding the picture of his late father — why did that slap stlll burn? Was it from the deep hurt feelings of a blow from a mother who hurt her child when he needed comfort? Was it anger from such a blow? Was it shame for the father, the cheek burning in the name of the life force in the face of a taken life? Had the mother been slapped a ritual blow by her own mother, when her first period came — the blow said to put a permanent bloom in a woman's cheek? The wine goes down, slowly, and lightly flushes the faces at the table. Then someone says, She did it to save his life, to keep him from following the father's path. She did it to waken him to danger — to say, This handsome man did a terrible thing to himself, and to you, to me. The mother is willing to do the awful thing of raising her hand to her son in order that he may live a long, nourishing, life-giving life. In whose else poems are the exactness and mystery of the spirit embodied so precisely and clearly in the flesh of the words? Stanley's music is like a miracle — or like an actual event or place in nature — God's poems! When I first read "The Portrait," I was struck with its plainsong, the iron ring of its primary bells: mother, father, kill, public, look. And then my heart was opened by the poem's longing empathy for the lost one — brave, deep, level. Kunitz wisdom, Kunitz passion, Kunitz accuracy and balance. His is our forbear, and yet his is the freshest voice.

Stanley Moss

A HISTORY OF COLOR

What is heaven but the history of color,
dyes washed out of laundry, cloth and cloud,
mystical rouge, lipstick, eye shadows? Harlot nature,
explain the color of tongue, lips, nipples,
against Death come ons of labia, penis, the anus,
explain how Christian gold and blue tempt the kneeling,
how Moslem green is miraculous in the desert,
how the personification of the rainbow is Iris,
the mother of Eros, why *Adam* in Hebrew
comes out of the redness of earth.

The cosmos and impatiens I planted this June
may outlast me, these yellow, pink and blue annuals
do not sell indulgences, a rose ravishes a rose.
The silver and purple pollen that has blown on the roof
of my car concludes a sacred conversation.

Against Death the concupiscent color wheels
of insects and birds, washerwomen and philosophers
sought a fixative for colors to replace unstable substances
like saliva, urine, and blood, the long process of boiling,
washing, and rinsing.   It is Death who works
with clean hands and a pure heart. Against him
Phoenician red-purple dyes taken from sea snails, the colors
fixed by exposing wool to air of the morning seas near Sidon,
or the sunlight and winds on the limestone cliffs of Crete—all lost,
which explains a limestone coastline
changed into mountains of pink-veined marble,
the discarded bodies of gods.

Of course Phoenician purple made for gods
and heroes cannot be produced nowadays.
Virgil thought purple was the color of the soul— all lost.
Anyone can see the arithmetic when purple
was pegged to the quantity and price of seashells.

Remember
the common gray and white seagull looked down
at the Roman Republic, at the brick-red and terra-cotta
dominant after the pale yellow stone of the Greek world,
into the glare of the Empire's white marble.
The sapphire and onyx housefly that circled
the jeweled crowns of Byzantium buzzed prayers,
remembers what it remembers.
The churches held Jesus dead and his weeping mother,
an empty tomb. In holy light and darkness
the presence of Christ was cupped in silver.
Death holds, whether you believe Christ
is there before you or not, you will not see Him later—
sooner prick the night sky with a needle to find the moon.

I fight Death with peppermints, a sweet to recall
the Dark Ages before the word *orange* existed.
In illuminated manuscripts St. Jerome,
his robes *egg-red*, is seen translating in the desert,
a golden lion at his feet—
or he is tied to a column naked in a dream,
flagellated for reading satires and Pliny's
Natural History that describes
the colors used by Apelles, the Greek master,
in a painting of grapes so true to life
birds would alight on them to feed.
Death, you tourist, you've seen it all and better before,
your taste: whipped saints sucking chastity's thumb,
while you eat your candy of diseased and undernourished infants.

On an afternoon when death seemed no more than a newspaper
in a language I could not read, I remember
looking down at Jerusalem from the Mount of Olives,
that my friend said: "Jerusalem is a harlot
everyone who passes leaves a gift."
Do birds of prey sing madrigals?
Outside the walls of Jerusalem, the crusaders
dumped mounts of dead Muslims
and their green banners, the severed heads of Jews,
some still wrapped in prayer-shawls,
while the Christian dead sprawled near the place of a skull
which is called in Hebrew *Golgotha.*
Among the living, blood and blood soaked prayers,
on the land of God's broken promises—a flagged javelin
stuck into the Holy Sepulcher as into a wild boar.

Hauled back by the *Franks*, colors never seen in Europe,
wonders of Islam, taffetas, organdies, brocades, damasks.
Gold threaded cloth that seemed made for the Queen of Heaven
was copied in Italy on certain paintings of Our Lady,
on her blue robes in gold in Arabic:
There is no God but God, Muhammad is His messenger—
for whom but Death to read.
Wrapped in a looted prayer rug,
an idea seized by Aquinas: the separation of faith and reason.
Later nicked from the library of Baghdad:
the invention of paper brought from China
by pilgrims on a hajj, looted rhyme, lenses,
notes on removing cataracts.
Certain veils would be lifted from the eyes of Europe,
all only for Death to see.

Within sight of Giotto's white, green and pink marble bell-tower
that sounded the promise of Paradise,

plants and insects were used for dyes made from oak gall,
bastard saffron, beetle, canary weed, cockroach,
the fixative was fermented piss from a young boy
or a man drunk on red wine, while the painters
mixed their pigments with egg yolks and albumen,
gold with lime, garlic, wax, and casein
that dried hard as adamantine, buffed with a polished agate
or a wolf's tooth.

At the time of the Plague, while the dead
lay unattended in the streets of Europe,
the yellow flag hung out more often than washing,
someone cloistered wrote a text
on making red from cinnabar, saffron from crocus,
each page an illuminated example.
At the Last Supper the disciples sat dead at table.
Does it matter to heaven if a sleeve is blue or red or black?
In Venice Titian found adding lead-white to azurite-blue
changed a blue sleeve to satin.
Still, by the late fifteenth century
color was seen as ornament,
almost parallel to the colors of rhetoric,
blue was moving away from its place describing
the vaults of heaven to the changing sky of everyday.

I think the absence of color is like a life without love.
A master can draw every passion with a pencil, but light,
shadow and dark cannot reveal the lavender Iris
between the opened thighs of a girl still almost a child,
or before life was through with her, the red and purple
pomegranate at the center of her being.

Against Death on an English day Newton discovered
a single ray of white light refracted,
decomposed into a spectrum of colors,

that he could reconstruct the totality,
mischievously reverse the process
and produce white light again—which perhaps is why
last century, in a painting by Max Ernst,
the Holy Mother is spanking the baby Jesus.

Goethe found a like proof on a sunny summer day—
the birds, I suppose, as usual devouring insects
courting to the last moment of life.
While sitting by a crystal pool watching
soldiers fishing for trout, the poet was taken
by spectrums of color refracted from a ceramic shard
at the bottom of the pool, then from the tails of swimming trout
catching fire and disappearing,
until a rush of thirsty horses, tired and dirtied by war,
muddied the waters.

A heroic tenor sings to the exploding sun:
every war is a new dawning—Fascist music.
Death would etch Saturn devouring his children on coins,
if someone would take his money.
Of course his I O U is good as gold.

Turner had sailors lash him to the mast
to see into a storm, then he painted slavers
throwing overboard the dead and dying,
sharks swimming through shades of red—
lashed to the mast, as Odysseus had himself lashed
not to hear the sirens sing how he would be remembered.
Later he painted the atheist Avalanche, then heaven
in truthful colors: Rain, Steam, Speed.
Portraits of nothing and very like, they said, *tinted steam.*
Of course Turner kept his paintings for himself,
his Burning of the Houses of Parliament.

Against oblivion a still life of two red apples.
It is like a beautiful woman. On her shoulder
the bruise of a painter's brush—she is no more
than a still life of peasant shoes.
You will not keep apples or shoes or France, Death says.
A child chooses an object first for color,
then for form, his first encounter with Death,
mother and father, aunts and uncles,
all the relatives of being.

Now this coloratura moves off-stage
to the present, which is a kind of intermission.
My friend Mark Rothko painted a last canvas,
gray and yellow, then took a kitchen knife, half cut off his wrists
bound and knotted behind his back,
(a trick of the spirit Houdini never mastered),
to throw off Eros, who rode his back and whipped him
even after he was dead, till Eros, the little Greek,
was covered with blood of the Song of Songs.
Now Rothko is a study of color, a purple chapel,
a still river where he looks for his mother and father.

Death, you tourist with too much luggage,
you can distinguish the living from your dead.
Can you tell Poseidon's trident from a cake fork,
the living from the living,
winter from summer, autumn from spring?
In a sunless world, even bats nurse their young,
hang upside down looking for heaven,
make love in a world where the lion, afraid of no beast,
runs in terror from a white chicken. Such are your winnings.
Death, I think you take your greatest pleasure
in watching us murdering in great numbers
in ways even you have not planned.
They say in paradise every third thought is of earth
and a woman with a child at her breast.

Stanley Moss

SONG FOR STANLEY KUNITZ

Creature to creature,
two years before we met
I remember I passed his table
at the Cedar Tavern.
He who never knew his father
seemed to view all strangers
as his father's good ghost,
any passing horse as capable
of being Pegasus, or pissing
in the street.
I who knew my father
was wary of any tame raccoon
with claws and real teeth.

At our first meeting forty years ago,
before the age of discovery,
I argued through the night
against the tragic sense of life;
I must have thought God wrote in spit.

I keep a petrified clam, his gift, on my desk.
These gray rings and layers of stone,
shape of a whale's eye, are old as any desert.
Measured against it, the morning, the Hudson River
outside my window are modern and brash,
the star of David, the cross, the hand of Fatima,
are man-made weather vanes.
My clamstone has weight and lightness.
It is my sweet reminder that flesh,

perhaps love, can remain in the natural world
long as poetry, tides, phases of the moon.
Tomorrow I shall wear it in my right eye,
a monocle for my talk on the relationship
between paleontology and anthropology.

Bless Celia, the cat of his middle years,
with her ribbons and hats, her pagan smile.
Bless the bobcat that was his in boyhood,
that killed a police dog in battle
on Main Street, Worcester, lost a foot for it
and had to be shot. A child with a leaf in his head,
he walked through Scabious Devilsbit,
Marshrag wort, Vernal grass
until the meadows wept. Bless his first garden,
his bird feeder still there after 81 years.
Did any of his long forgotten kindnesses
alter history a little?

What a *Luftmensch* he might have been,
his feet barely touching Commercial Street,
dancing home at three in the morning
with an ocean of money!
But how could he face the moon, or the land
beside his house without a garden? Unthinkable.
I think what is written
in roses, iris and trumpet vine
is read by the Lord God.
Such a place of wild and ordered beauty,
is like a heart that takes on the sorrows
of the world . . . He translates into all tongues.

Lucille Clifton

FLOWERS

here we are
running with the weeds
colors exaggerated
pistils wild
embarrassing the calm family flowers   oh
here we are
flourishing for the field
and the name of the place
is Love

Lucille Clifton

if i stand in my window
naked in my own house
and press my breasts
against my windowpane
like black birds pushing against glass
because i am somebody
in a New Thing

and if the man come to stop me
in my own house
naked in my own window
saying i have offended him
i have offended his

Gods

let him watch my black body
push against my own glass
let him discover self
let him run naked through the streets
crying
praying in tongues

Mary Oliver

SNOWY NIGHT

Last night, an owl
in the blue dark
tossed
an indeterminate number

of carefully shaped sounds into
the world, in which,
a quarter of a mile away, I happened
to be standing.

I couldn't tell
which one it was—
the barred or the great-horned
ship of the air—

it was that distant. But, anyway,
aren't there moments
that are better than knowing something,
and sweeter? Snow was falling,

so much like stars
filling the dark trees
that one could easily imagine
its reason for being was nothing more

than prettiness. I suppose
if this were someone else's story
they would have insisted on knowing
whatever is knowable— would have hurried

over the fields
to name it—the owl, I mean.
But it's mine, this poem of the night,
and I just stood there, listening and holding out

my hands to the wild glitter
falling through the air. I love this world—
but not for its answers.
And I wish good luck to the owl,

whatever its name—
and I wish great welcome to the snow,
whatever its severe and comfortless
and beautiful meaning.

Reetika Vazirani

LETTER TO THE MOOR

How could I not see you
in my father's house evenings
you came for dinner and to talk
about wars. I loved heroics.
                    But don't you know
                    they are mine too.
         If I speak of this bluntly

they'll call me Bianca's twin, drunk
on cheap infatuation, a whore.
I have no words to limn interior
                    climates. Nights. My arm
                    clutches your dark brightness —
         your arm on my paler one.

What are these skins if not ourselves?
One husband, one wife; that is how I see
our marriage. But we say
                    moons need pitch to be seen.
                    Midnight needs the moon
         to stitch its cloak of wonders.

Living. What combinations.
Two skins and one per citizen. In books
black is beast. I'm Mary, alabaster,
                    I'm the virgin dewlike
                    morning flush. A flat world
         but I roamed it hungrily.

From limb to limb I climbed men
in my mind, suitor after
suitor, next in line for Brabantio's
              daughter: men smiled: we
              talked of our childhoods
       in Venice. I *felt nothing*

So let them call me a whore, say I deceived,
call you pornographic. Who conquered
whom, and what's the war now?
              A wolf's wish for days —
              for this hunger to keep
       alighting and your grip

to catch my skin's stark shattering.
Break my fall, I give it all up to you.
And if I wished heaven
              made me a man, I
              take back the words.
       I've given everything

to keep me as I am. Go
now — I'll keep missing you like strong weather.
I have your handkerchief of strawberries.
              I won't cry. Fierce
              holds have their ways.
       I'll outlast the ancient,

jealous disapprovals. What bred them?
I'll wait out storms and floods and flight
delays. I have one wish, call it
              what you will love,
              I call it a life.

Reetika Vazirani

ENGLISH

Their army barracks were fun in the jungle
outside Lucknow, wide paths to tan buildings,
and men wore caps with quarter-moon fronts.
I wondered, do caps keep the moon from shining in?
What do they think of ours — we have
a hundred names, a hundred phases,
and in England there's just moon, that's all.
And I think of the quick words they used —
Hello. Cheers. Thank you very much old chap.
Little words from a locked box
and the twenty-six letters, so few.

In the canteen, I saw folded napkin,
fork-knife-spoon, cloth and glass
and gin-water, gin-tonic, gin-soda;
eating places off in squares like flower beds
at Christ's Church, headstone, footstone,
grass between. Then the General, he said *Neat,*
and a bearer brought a clear drink on a tray.
The silver cutlery clicked on the plates,
words like a store-keeper's coins.
I didn't want to leave, but at thirteen hundred sharp
we filed out by a hundred olive quarter-moon caps.

The soldiers made paths through the jungle
to let light in and wore caps to keep it out,
and officers drove at noon while we sat
in the shade. My uncle, a General,
said they are great adventurers,

their own country is an island.
And when I said *island* it was a mint leaf
on my tongue, an almond slice,
a moon with its thin rays on the windowpane.

Reetika Vazirani

BEIJING

Mao wanted to get rid of birds
because of the droppings,
then bugs took over and ate trees.
You leave the Forbidden City
single file, and the earth is so loose
it whirls at the gates. It is everywhere.
Trees are the only way to tame it.
Meanwhile where are they, dogs and cats?
Dust rises and storms around you.
No birds but bats. The earth,
its only home a watery eye.

Paul Muldoon

HARD DRIVE

With my back to the wall
and a foot in the door
and my shoulder to the wheel
I would drive through Seskinore.

With an ear to the ground
and my neck on the block
I would tend to my wound
in Belleek and Bellanaleck.

With a toe in the water
and a nose for trouble
and an eye to the future
I would drive through Derryfubble

and Dunnamanagh and Ballynascreen,
keeping that wound green.

Cleopatra Mathis

OLD TRICK

Spring wants me back,
and I should know better than to heed
that old hag, the goddess
disguising herself with the first green
she can muster. Her true self hanging around,
gray, icy, bent, gazing from the corners
while I glory in the fine scribble
skimming the trees. I let her
bear the weight of my heart,
not my first mistake: every year she promises

to bring back what I love, and for awhile
she does—a flower here, another there,
fast-talking me through the price
I'll pay later. It's one panorama
followed by the next, the returning
birds in a parade, finches
twittering at dawn. They too

make you think you can trust them:
look at those nests, their faith
at your feeder, but I can tell you this,
keep an eye on the children.
September will come, the ripe business
whirring—everything
you can't see in all the greenery,
its constancy already tinged: a slight cast,
a whine. Your own girl will vanish
under that yellowing wing.

Cleopatra Mathis

CUTLERY

You must earn the fork,
but only after you've earned
the spoon. All you'll know
of the knife
is the blade you remember,
cousin to the fork's five prongs,
those scissored lines
you dragged along your arm.
Points for the healing,
points to earn anything
hell-bent for damage.
Nothing's innocent, not
in this world. You'll eat
like the civilized only before
dismissal through the double
metal door. Ignore that bell
from the other side: the visitor
you'll have to earn as well.
You're the zero
on heaven's chart.
Nothing's for you
but this plate of white food.
Two fingertips and one thumb
will make a clever tool.
Hungry enough, you'll slave
to institutional hours.
It's twelve: you eat,
at one you'll speak.

Don't want to eat?
Don't want to speak?
We'll have to put you all alone
in the metal bed in the metal room
with all the metal lights
turned out. Pound,
and stirrups will hold you down.
Scream, and it's double
time, twice the fear
that makes you open up the scabs
in the Solitay Room, where you hear
the little voice of the one
that brought you,
the one that won't quit
breathing in your ear.

Cleopatra Mathis

WHAT TO TIP THE BOATMAN?

Delicate—the way at three she touched
her hands tip to tip, each finger a rib
framing the tepee of her hands.
So tentative that joining, taking
tender hold of her body, as if the ballast
of her selfhood rested there. Already
she could thread tiny beads through the eye
and onto string, correctly placing
each letter of her name, sorting
thin black lines to make an alphabet,
the needle just so in her little hand.
She loved that necklace less
than cat's cradle, a game to weave
the strand through forefinger, ringfinger, pinkie.
She could lace a basket, a boat
that could even carry water. *What to tip
the boatman?* I asked, trying to amuse her
with church and steeple turned to my empty palm.
Naptime, she'd lie there making shapes
above her, signing the air.

Later I saw the light touch in those twinned
fingertips had become her way
of holding still, keeping balance.
She had reached home before I did, finding
no mother at the bus stop, and entered
the silenced house for the first time alone.
Ancient, venerable, the whole place
waited, a relative with smells and creaks

she hesitated to greet. When I found her
she had made her way to the formal great room,
polite center of the hectic house where even
the clock's old thud gave back the heart
of simple waiting. Good guest, a shadow
on the rose Victorian settee, she sat,
her hands precise before her, an offering.

Bruce Smith

SWEETS

A sob in the body, late August, white time and counter-miracle
to the music on the radio, "Struttin' with some Barbecue," the mighty
arpeggios and silent halleluias from our satchelmouthed hero.

The time crossed like light with something old like the tabernacle
and its illicit opposite that remembers fondly the flavors of captivity —
the vinegar and sugar and love-poisoned tomato.

Only a voice could join the mercy and the rightful
and it wasn't yours, it was the unearthly
singer from the dirty south, who had the moan

that was your mother's ash-hauling eye roll
and your father's speaking in tongues. The authority
of the voice was burn for burn, word for word ratio

that meant we could remember the shackles
and the foreskin of the heart removed and be ready
for the call through the scat and the bruised tempos

where everyone heard something and was enthralled.
Everyone was a girl or a boy at school, fidgety,
and then comes the nudge, the unh, and the ecstasy, O

then the season had an angel
clearing his throat and your shitty little history
was okay, somehow, was solo after solo.

Bruce Smith

WHITE GIRL, ALABAMA

I came home to Alabama from a spot
where a singing, dancing mouse ran an amusement park

and in my state there was a bus boycott
a seamstress fingered with the "segregator"

and the "little niggers" walked and the "big niggers"
talked in the paper of Gandhi and Reinhold Niebuhr

whoever they were, besides, we didn't take the bus.
My secrets were skin and what inside was

for a boy, imagining that, and God the Negro
preacher said would fill his belly with Jim Crow.

It was an open, red-mouthed summer
that smelled of brine, or I did, I was not clever,

I was merely alive in a peach dress
and dry unlike the wet-with-knowledge one the seamstress

wore. I had a heart and it was angry
and it was uppity and it was a townie

heart compared to my sister's who boo-hooed
hers through the phone from the University in Tucsaloosa.

My lips swelled. My heart swelled in my chest
(I couldn't call them breasts)

and in my legs and arms. I pinwheeled through
the noisy brightness of the blue voodooed

with pins of rain.
My sister had problems that were men

I wanted too, a movie sort of thing
or a song, unwritten, unrehearsed, thrilling

that turned a mica-flecked mud if I gave it thought
like mixing brown and white and buckshot and the light.

Where was the place I could go that wasn't all
summer, our way of life, or animal?

I waited inside, then inside the inside. Close
like a closet in the thunder, there to *dis-close*

(I sometimes thought in words instead of pressures
on the skin) what would be the cure

or ransom of the country
which meant my plain faced "fokes," that kind of country,

and the dark citizens of Tuskeegee
and the conspiracy of places ruled by Kennedy —

the country. I woudn't let him in my pants.
That summer we added in your pants

to everything until it wasn't a joke
but the picket fence and gate of the unspoken

laws. Or between the sheets
we tacked on between the sheets

to the names of songs, "Come Softly to Me . . . "
between the sheets. I wanted lovers or enemies

and I got fleas and dreams between the sheets
where the music mingled with klavern and heat

lightning and self-kisses
and the sprinklers hiss.

Gail Mazur

DANA STREET, DECEMBER

(for Stanley Kunitz)

As if I had no language
and would begin again
in the linguistics
of infancy,
but amnesiac
therefore with nothing
to say—

(unlike the woman in rehab
who could walk,
and walked the linoleum
at all hours, shouting
to no one, I KNOW
THE WORDS! I KNOW THE WORDS!

—all the words
she knew)

I walked,
past a yard
overgrown, scraggly
after the first frost,
a rose——the bitterest orange——
still blooming, piercing
the morning

(My work had stopped,
I thought
forever)

—perfection
or imperfection
not the issue, a radiance
utterly itself,
pale petals tinged
fiery (provident neighbor,
astute, to nurture
that gift)

(I didn't take it)

Not to be thinking
Is this enough, this
moment, the chilled
unpromising air,
not to be wanting more
than I'd been given,
but remembering

last October when
I carried a glass vase,
its rose,
lush, creamy,
across my living room
for your appreciations,

how you rose from
the rush-seated chair
to meet it, saying,
"Oh no, Gail,
the *rose* doesn't come

to you—
you go
to the rose."

Peter Balakian

PHOTOSYNTHESIS

The slips of the day-
lilies come off.

The wind blows
in from Vermont,
blows the silk kimonos

off the delphiniums,
blows the satin cowls
off the jack-in-the-pulpits.

Let it blow
the detonated-pollen
green, acid-rubbed,

plumed and rotting day—
blow into the leaves

their silver undersides
wet you at night.

Slide your tongue
into the green dark

so you can see the ultra-
violet scars on the goldfields
where the bees come in the day.

The night air rises
like steam
from a mud-pot,

and you see nothing.
Hear no voice.
See no light.

Just yourself
staring back at you
in middle age,

as if the novocain
of the sea urchin
froze your lids.

You see the window
you built

where you placed your hands
and broke your turquoise jars
and saw the stones

of scalding yellow
where the steam had burned
things back to where your private lust

and your longing for history
were colorless, and the blood
of the dianthus was gone.

You see your life rise
and slide away like steam,

feel a goat-tongue
lost in a mountain
wet you down.

Grace Schulman

BLUE DAWN

I see Viola float in on a plank
from the wreck, touch land, pocket a seashell
for luck, and, shivering, glide into a kingdom,

as once Long Island's settlers trudged ashore
and, though weary, took in blue-green forests
at sunrise, before lines furrowed the oak trees.

When his ship steamed into New York Harbor,
my father stood on deck in cramped, thin shoes
and watched blue rocks grow to be Ellis Island.

Sailing through fog at daybreak, his eyes burning
with the statue's unlit torch, how could he know
that one day he would walk on asphalt pavement

wearing a tweed coat, though still in cramped shoes.
Scant time for shops, he said, but I knew he chose
to save the blue wonder of what might be,

as I do now: slate flagstones going blue
in the not-yet-risen sun, an unopened iris,
the miracle of a lined, unwritten page.

Grace Schulman

IN THE CAFÉ

Blue notes like words cry out to one another.
Harsh trumpet phrases, open-horn — like rage
dug into earth, then risen to huge tones —

vault the night air, and, muted, fall.
At bedtime, Father read a poem in Polish,
lines memorized and chanted. There were trumpets

and bells in his voice that held back the night
with wizard-talk I never understood,
words that told secrets, padlocks to pry open,

spells against the dark. My father learned them
from his brother, Jan, who cursed hunger in song,
and who was found at last on a dirt road

beaten, frozen, dead. Father fled Poland
and seldom spoke of Jan, but still I heard,
under his satin tones, Jan's mockery,

blue trumpet notes that sang to one another,
secrets that unfurled like silver waves
far out at sea. Then traveled closer, closer.

Grace Schulman

POEM ENDING WITH A PHRASE FROM THE PSALMS

Here where loss spins the hickory's dry leaves,
rolls miles under wheels, and bleaches reeds
that shone wine-red, I invoke a rose
still rising like a choir, past its prime
on a spindly bush that bore scarce blooms,
as I wake to hear a jay screech like a gate
swung open, and see your hand enfolding mine
on linen: *teach us to number our days*.

Michael Ryan

REMINDER

Torment by appetite
is itself an appetite
dulled by inarticulate,
dogged, daily

loving-others-to-death—
as Chekhov put it, "compassion
down to your fingertips"—,
looking on them as into the sun

not in the least for their sake
but slowly for your own
because it causes
the blinded soul to bloom

like deliciousness in dirt,
like beauty from hurt,
their light—*their* light—
pulls so surely. Let it.

Michael Ryan

EVERY SUNDAY

Psychotic homeless boy
blocking our exit from the church—
straggle-haired, bloated,
eyes shining like ice—

doing his rooster-pecking thing
with his hand made the beak
into each of our faces
as we file out—

or is it snake-striking
or airhole-punching
or just compulsive counting us
one and one and one?

He will not live long.
He will allow the pastor
to wrap an arm around his shoulder,
and lead him to coffee and crullers.

But to *be* him

Elise Asher

CYCLE

The day is inconsequential, my love,
it seems inconsequence exists for us;
rare days in whose ample laps of light
we sit on wood and stare
while hollow chimes parade along our nerves.
You leafing the pages of an austere book
and I caught in the nooks of insect intimacy.
And at the rear of the long march, the chimes
reaffirm our wedding: we interlock our fingers
for the ritualistic walking in to dine.

And meanwhile love is fretting in the eaves
with folded wings: myself and you entwined,
lodged up there in one combined complaint
high above our hearts this timid hive.
Yet we compel such far-off tinkling
to sound felicitous as ancient temple bells
over the vast inconsequence of living,
our intimate forgiving.

Elise Asher

WALKING AFTER A RAINSTORM

Who walks now
wears the world
Purling in prayer:
sea-shell
pressed to ear,
womb-psalm unknown
to dream or memory.

Who walks now
becomes leaf and bark
and heart of tree
glistening with rain
and worm-sodden air.

Who walks now
is a world walking
a fractional span
in purity,

a walking world
of purity.

Who walks now
is Holy.

Dannie Abse

SNAPSHOT OF RUSKIN IN VENICE

That man now coming out of the Hotel
will soon be Art's spy, happily disguised,
a long black cloth over his head, taking
daguerrotypes. High up, he'll measure
and draw and pry, assent to the savagery
of the Gothic. Venetians, below, passing by
will gaze at this headless figure surprised.

On Sunday in church with pious Effie
he kneeled beside decaying candles.
The drone and moan of Latin resembled grief.
The chunky priest in his sable and satin
had not heard the geologists' hammers
destroying the pages of the Bible.
Not for him the abyss of disbelief.
Rather the old rudimentary fable
where God consoles and the Devil rages.

And last night in the marble ballroom
a spunky clan of competing officers
frontally displayed their peacock's tail
for Effie — her eyes dancing above the fan.
Eros in handcuffs and without his wit.
Where the barrel organ and the monkey?

Flirty Australians! Their waltzes and their polkas!
Well, let her have her fling. But party over,
chandelier-blind, stumbling into dark,
her foot so light in the ballroom clumsily

crushed a snail — the spinal noise of it!
And she who'd been so vivacious cried.

Tittle-tattle, now this feminine thing
wearisome. Limply, he tried to comfort her
who needed to be more than gently kissed.
'Please, Effie dear,' wondering helplessly
was it the silly snail that made her weep?

Soon, bonded, they boarded their gondola
but, above, a shackle gargoyle laughed.
He looked up, saw the stone leer and higher
a crazed star fall and fall from the jail
of the sky making its bid for freedom.

Dannie Abse

FLY

He was talking about Kierkegaard
when I observed a housefly had chosen
to settle on his elegant left shoe.

He was saying how we are a mixture
of the finite and the infinite
unaware of this fly, a masterpiece.

He was saying we are a synthesis
of the temporal and the eternal
while the fly's proboscis sucked his shoe.

And when it crawled on to his exposed sock
I thought how the female domesticus,
programmed, lays its eggs in refuse or dung;

how the larvae, those small white maggots,
change to pupae without casting their skins
till eight days later the perfect fly emerges.

Stephen Berg

FLEAS

(for Stanley Kunitz)

" . . . loss of their friends, expecting that themselves
should be summoned the next hour." London
1665, but not now, not here, plague
of another kind, tell me what it is
as Oedipus visited by one
decided to root out the murderer,
the cause, rid the city of it, cure,
I mean these days there seems to be a fear
of what? take your mind in your hands
like an apple, explain the moon
to the rat I saw last night in the street
scuttling under a car, better yet
touch everyone you've ever loved who isn't
here anymore, see them in shafts of light.

Stephen Berg

LIKE SINGING

True too this belief, though flesh though blood
though bones and breath, in something other than
the hunger of the leaf
to be leaf, the root's lust to be root, vine
winding itself upward into its tip
and how a man gets up each day as if
nothing he knows decides, guides, takes him where
he goes: see me, rescue me with your eyes,
speak to me, don't use words
"so void was I of everything that was good"
a man sits in a chair and writes these words
and no one hears them yet except that man—
can't a man know more than the world of things
can't a man break through the little he knows

Stephen Berg

*

I could hear who in the walls, the floors, some
presence even Aristotle might not
be able to name, "touch-object" "taste object"
in the interminable analysis
that's triggered when the soul
seeks, gropes, flees— last night I woke
at 4 & at least momentarily—
empty mouth that prays to become
whatever it is not, whatever it
pretends it needs to feed on to become
mind beyond mind beyond
wakes middle of the night and can't
touch anyone not even itself can't feel
where it is who it is why what it is

Mark Rudman

BICOASTAL: BOBBY DARIN AT THE COPA

(for my fathers)

In the summer of my sixteenth year, my stepfather
got a pulpit in Beverly Hills he would have loved
to have been permanent: Rabbi to the stars.
We rented a furnished pad on Sunset Strip
where many an afternoon it was the singer Jack
Jones and me alone at the pool,
only Jack's deck chair was surrounded
by an entourage: agents, managers, vocal coaches,
toupees, gold chains, Hawaiian shirts,
who yakked and gesticulated with cigars as batons
about his current gig at the Coconut Grove,
analyzing his previous night's performance
for what should be kept, what dropped;
and I thought what a good singer he was—

("though not as good," both fathers agreed,
"as his father, Allan Jones, the tenor")—
but that onstage he lacked the personal touch
of Bobby Darin at the Copa when he stepped down
and mingled among the audience and sang "Dream
Lover" to a golden-haired little girl
who would have been in kindergarten,
and asked in a tender and intimate voice
"How old are you darlin'?"
and "Is the room too smoky for you?"
My father'd consented to take me to see
Darin at the Copa, because he'd read that the kid

could really sing unlike the others
he considered goons with pompadours
who depended on echo chambers and tricks.

Peter Davison

TASTING THE FIRE

"Practically no vibrating body produces a pure sound."
                                        –Harvard Dictionary of Music

He ambles without crankiness,
            meditates absently but keenly,
                        forgets

nothing. Some can recall when his
            harsh fist bruised the table; others, when he
                        was heard, in fact, to whine.

Yet he has not shied from his changes,
            trolling deep
                        to encompass all

the graveled and sanguinary territory he
            had nosed through. Musing
                        late, after

the sear of martinis and the turmoil of an
            overspiced dinner, he outfaces
                        sleep until his wits wake

and carry him to the shapely
            chamber of imagination, with its eerie
                        light that is unveiled at peril

of blindness. Over the decades his grip has
        grown gentler, his voice has modulated to
                purer sound.

The tune he launches now,
        alone, alone,
                resonates through the upstream
                of his body's blood.

Hugh Seidman

SOMEBODY STAND UP AND SING

Today, the computer head hunter, as I have said.

Buzzed on Starbucks house blend among the brokers.

More and more: Father in the mirror (for better commerce).

Yesterday, masked revelers outside a building.
Imagine, unlimited identity.

No match for the laureates, I know—still, word opens.

> One night, one day.
> Weight into volume.
>
> Or is it:
> volume into weight?
>
> Herbert's line?:
> *absolute ear versus immense range.*

Or perhaps the marbled-library lecture.

It appears (one infers?)
Auden felt guilt like Vallejo's:

> *Someone passes by counting with his fingers.*
> *How speak of the not-*i *without screaming.*

Yes, caffeine edge.

Eyes open to piped-in guitar.
Something as if *ancient*.

Father's paradoxical neck cords in a too-tight white shirt.
Should not the corpse be getting thinner?

Suddenly, a woman's laugh:
like a backbone of pain,
like a child's duty never learned.

Vibrations of sound to dark, to light, to ever-widening dark.

So that I say,
as to anyone,
but to myself:
"Somebody stand up and sing."

Diana Der-Hovanessian

TELL THE ARMENIAN STORY

Tell the Armenian story in
black and white please.
We've had enough shades
of blood and red
and purple prose.
We've had enough amber
sunsets, hennaed tufa,
enough golden wheat.
Let's have some rest.
Tell the Armenian story
but not the gory past.
Let it remain buried
with the roots of poppies
on our plains. Let the blue
light of morning and the bright
greens of Karabagh remain
our secret. Keep the orange
flame of Dzidzanapert
and the yellow city sunsets
ours alone. Show the pink
and beige monasteries
and the citrus-shaded birds
all in shades of gray.
Don't show the violet mist
and blue snow of Ararat
nor the aquamarine Sevan
being gilt at sunrise.
Don't tint the apricot trees
with pink evening inks.

No gold or bottled green
in the valleys just silver
cold and bright. We do not
want the heart to break.
We want only light.

Alberto Ríos

SMALL RISINGS

The middle summer light in water
Coming through the window and rain
Makes new shadows on me,
Giving me appendages I had not seen—
A second nose,
A sixth finger.
They were no surprise.
I had suspected them and others
Since childhood,
Having seen if I moved my wrist quickly
Ten or twelve fingers on a single hand.
Two noses every day, one on my face
One in the mirror. I could touch
Each to each in a meeting of nostrils,
All four of them clearly mine.
The rain and its afternoon shadows
Give me what I already know.
Sometimes at night I get up
And from my bed I watch myself,
My other legs, the rising back of my head,
The tired intent to brush my hair.
I see myself go, that me
When I walk out the door.

Christopher Middleton

AN IMAGE IN THE HATCH

Now you wonder what they really looked like,
The two who for a moment only in the hatch—

And a bottle of sauce, asters, yellow,
Crowning the white vases, clustered beside

A sweating shiny metal jug of water
Between you and the profiles in the hatch—

Lingered for a moment, one who paid the bill,
Broad in the beam she spoke a word of Spanish,

The other who was dark, whose little dog tooth
Shone in the light of a single candle flame,

Waiting to take the money and be gone.
A dozen paces, at the most, between

The bar you sat at, and the dining room,
What were they like, those places? Who

Took them? Who did not, but stayed to see,
Framed in the hatch, the profiles and the candle,

The candle flame that lit the inexhaustible
Features of Madeleine in a canvas by Latour,

Lit the blonde who paid and little Laura,
Their semi-faces lit behind the water jug,

Behind the vases and the yellow asters,
Behind the slim sauce bottle on the hatch shelf.

The objects, then the faces, so triangulated
With memory of paintings, Dutch not only,

Opened penetrable space hither and yon;
Idea could construct, even before the objects

Assumed intelligence freely and appeared.
Idea could dance a thing alive into its orbit.

This differs from the peaches in Russia tearing
Two selves apart in the anxiety of an exile.

It differs from the music which is not a thing
But covers the ground before the thing enters the hatch.

It is the old, in a light that is half-hidden
As the faces were, a shadow of the potential

Consuming a cheek or a loose hank of hair;
It is the new intact, now coming into leaf.

It is not who, it is how such minimalia accord,
Accord when nobody need be there, but being there

You will have tasted flesh the courage comes from,
Agile, dispassionate, for the taking, yours.

Forrest Gander

TO THE INVISIBLE WORLD

At once, he rose from his seat, bared his right shoulder, set
his knee
on the floor and, respectfully folding his hands, addressed
them thus:

*The trace on my lips of her nipples' rouge improves the taste of
the wine.*

*Asleep, she is completely closed, windowless, contained by the
world in its dark
while also she illuminates some portion of that world, the por-
tion
where I remain, entranced.*

Thrash-polka on her radio, a bluegill on her line.

*To what can I compare her conversation?
Karl Jansky built an antenna to study shortwave interference
but he discovered radio galaxies.*

*From the light friction of her limbs when she walks,
the forest blooms beside her, berries ripen.*

*Her quick cries of pleasure and surprise.
I am held awake listening for their return.*

Her eyes constitute a disorder, a methodical perplexity.

Love solves nothing, though it has made me appear.

She is a prism through which light intensifies. Her voice, a
stringed paulownia.

Her great originality is her liveliness, an incessant bursting forth
of identification,
enthusiasm coincident with the forever ungraspable.

There was a groundswell of low murmuring. Then the head
monk called, *Next.*

Anne Marie Macari

SLOPE OF STONE AND DIRT

It wasn't the house I loved or later missed,
the house with its rotting foundations that seemed

so small when we climbed the hill,
like the winter morning my son and I looked back

to find it distant, padded with snow.
We turned then and rose onto rock ledge

almost tripping over a dead deer—heart the birds
came for, throat split, eyes open.

Not the house, but what sloped up from the back door:
green boulders, broken dogwood,

the pride-of-India that blew down the year after I left.
Not the rooms, which grew dank. Not

the floors I paced or what flew
down the halls. A house listens

then confesses everything. Pipes burst,
plaster buckles, mice scratch inside the walls where

some die and leave the bells of decay ringing, ringing.
Think of the fire in the kitchen

and how I stood—9 months pregnant—on a chair washing
black soot. Think of the end, someone

pounding doors, the malicious flights of stairs. The last time
I climbed my hill trying not to trample

the moss, I didn't know that what I'd miss was not the house
but the slope of stone and dirt, dead trees

fallen into beds of leaves, a half-gone paradise.
When I broke myself open

I could never go back. When I broke
I was an arrow in love with my life again: I was harsh,

stooped from the pain, enraged.

Arthur Gregor

PORTRAIT

A portrait of myself
of more than thirty years ago
bought by a friend
who willed it to a friend
who has willed it to me,
now hangs in my bedroom/study
facing my desk. Drawn in crayons,
the colors mostly subdued blues,
my head resting on the right hand,
often my pose when listening.
A pensive look; too sad, some say,
as if I knew then what I would see
in it now.   A long procession
of figures recede in the background
bright as in a surrealist painting,
my mother listening to an opera
affected by the lovers' fate
and I, in the same room with her,
helpless to console her.
A boyhood friend I had scorned,
another I had preferred who when we
were grown but hadn't met in years,
leaned over me as I sat
in a darkened theater
waiting for the film to start.
And so many others and events
all fixed in memory's compelling tones of
an unnamable happiness lost,

and the sights reflecting this,
as when even as a youth
I had sensed a desperate want
in figures embracing in a doorway
or disappearing behind shrubbery;
or when observing from my window
in a room across the courtyard
an aged father caring for
an adolescent daughter,
just the two of them at table behind
the undrawn curtain.
                                        Or years later
on travels, long journeys,
when on a walk by the sea
in the dim darkness I would spot the stranger
who would know me instantly,
would know why, a few steps away,
I would stop to look back.
What, in the end, are travels all about,
at least what have mine been all about
if not to regain, be close again
to that unspecified loss,
the promise of retrieval
contained in sceneries, vistas strongly marked,
from terraces high above sloping flowery fields,
from classical hillsides
possibilities for a union with
the great good gained
long before memory began,
long before the streets,
the dark and narrow, broad
and tree-lined streets
where I had been at home
were gone.

In the portrait, in its subdued blues
the artist caught in that wistful look
what I had to have learned too well
even by then, nothing lasts, nothing can.

                    The coasts recede,
swift, billowing clouds, the earth.
Not the confrontations, face to face
nor an accord of place—
deep in the bright far end
in the unchanging glow
solace gained alone remains, recoveries
for which travels were begun.

Joshua Weiner

PSALM

When I sing to you I am alone these days
 and can't believe it, as if the stars

—while gazing up at them—just shut off.
 Astonished:

I search out the one light, brightest light
 in the night sky, but find

I cannot find it without weaker lights to guide me
 like red tail-lights on a car up ahead

after midnight when I'm sleepy, that illustrate
 how the highway curves,

curving to a hook, and maybe save my life
 and it means nothing to me

because nothing has happened, not the faintest
 glint of drama.

(Raining gently, the tarmac turns slick, moistened
 to life with renewed residues;

I can sense it with my hands on the wheel,
 the drops—not too heavy—

drumming off-time rhythms on the metal roof,
 the metal surface like a skin tense and sweating

and the road empty now, there are so many
        exits . . .)

Where is my family, both hearth and constellated trail of
flicker
        I have always followed to your word?

There, but mastered by fear of dark compulsions
        and loathing atrocities committed in your name,

they hit the dimmer switch and extinguish themselves
        whenever I sing your praises . . .

Who can blame them?
        (I can't help but blame them.)

And anyway they are far from me
        (farthest when they come to visit)—

I should be self-reliant, in my armchair
        like Emerson reading by a single lamp;

I should not need them, finding in you
        myself, little firebug needing no outlet,

my soft light blinking as I oxidize my aimless flight
        to love, to the good,

even my glowing chemistry unnecessary now
        in the ultimate light of day.

But what good would that do me?
        With you, in you, perhaps others do not matter,

but this isn't heaven, and I cannot make a circle
  all on my own—

Photon, luciferin, meteor: as I burn myself
  to pieces, I only pray

let my sparking tail remain a moment longer
  than our physics might allow,

some indication, however brief, that there continues
  (amen) a path to follow.

Bodhan Boychuck

AFTER READING "HORNWORM"

A butterfly
lit a branch
of the bird-cherry tree
and took off.

I gathered
light from that branch
to my palm
and peered into it
untill I perceived myself
a butterfly

on God's
hand.

Shirley Kaufman

A SHEET OF FOIL

First day of spring on the Hill of Anemones, masses of scarlet,
pink and deep purple, the blood of Adonis seeping
into the earth. Hatched by the sun, they widen their mouths
and tilt backwards to take the light in, fields brimming
all the way to the village on the next hill. Wildflowers,
stones, everything warming in its ancient bed. Even
the chill between us. My mother smiles, I nod my head
to acknowledge the endlessness of the dead. To let her know

I remember we sat on the floor together while she cut the wings
and glued them on cardboard and fastened them to my shoulders.
Shimmering gold foil. I was the angel she pasted in scrapbooks.
She goes on turning the pages without me. Sometimes
I find myself in a room I've entered forgetting what for.
Or I could say each place I return to is changed. That's why
the slope in front of the house I grew up in was steeper before.
When I spread my arms at the top of our stairs, I flew.

Grow old along with me! The best is yet to be. My mother read me
her favorite poem from the leather-bound gilt-edged book
her first love gave her. The leather was green as pine boughs,
soft as my pillow when I pressed my finger in it. I could feel
his breath on her skin. So this was poetry. I heard the music
as if from the throats of flowers, angels sirens mermaids mother
singing next to my father while he drove, *All of me, why not take
all of me?* Bel canto with a little kvetch. Her eyes were cinnamon,

blurry with tears the day I caught her over my diary, and bellowed
my hate. Fifteen and furious, her only child crazy with breasts,
she like a creeper, fastening. Nechama. Her name meant comfort.
Not in the doctors' waiting rooms. Not in the cigar smoke
sanctum of his poker nights. Not in her anguish of pleasing.
But there in the picture between her sisters holding me on the
canvas swing. Tender and blameless. We rock in the backyard
under the willow. Comfort ye, comfort ye, says the prophet.

When I walk in the dry river bed, the crunch of my sandals
is the sound of childhood, running along the beach in summer.
Surf at the edge, like the swish of a thin sheet of foil
as it wrinkles and folds on itself. She keeps smoothing it out.
This isn't my childhood, and I move here cautious under the steep
cliffs, the layers of sediment. The way I walk between
closely packed graves, not to profane what's under them.
Not to disturb her fingers at my back, steadying the wings.

Shirley Kaufman

All over Rehavia there are
tiny gardens green on the corners
in somebody's memory
                        the name
incised on a concrete slab
                        and a bench
with two immovable doves

blooms are staggered
                        even in winter
when cyclamen jiggle the earth
and then the freesias

stopping to rest at the end
of my block
            two elderly women
stare straight ahead
without speaking
                    hands folded
under their elbows

                    coming undone
a little
        like braided straw
from too much handling
                        too many
losses in Europe
                or here

wind bruises
            their delicate foreheads

their skin
the color of water
on sand
when summer is over
the shore
undazzled
and all the children
have gone back to school

Allison Funk

HEART'S-EASE

Weathervane heart spinning, horse and driver,
how will they get home, rain turning to ice
on the back roads of Indiana?

An itinerant preacher
traveling from one soul to the next. East,
west, fouled compass—

the tired horse lifts her feet
and the man tries to remember his God
that lately he's taken to calling

by the name of a flower
he's heard of.
Where does it blossom? he wonders,

far now from his children,
where they're sitting, he prays,
round the table saying the blessing.

Then Helen or Esther (whose turn *is* it tonight?)
will rise to recite from the Bible. Lord,
the words coming to mind, all

the Reverend can think of, back wheels stuck
in the muddy ruts, is what a boy, a guest
of one of his children, completely unchurched,

muttered when called upon for a verse.
A rolling stone gathers no moss. Jesus!
he cries out, striking his horse, despairing

of the barn, ever putting his harness up,
where *does* it thrive? Heart's-ease,
that flower the blessed also call love-in-idleness.

                    In memory of George Knox (1852-1912)

Nick Flynn

INSIDE NOTHING

A sun-fed engine, the inside

constant, a flower taken
whole. In winter our wings

move faster, to keep the sun
inside, inside nothing

& we fill the nothing with suns,

line them up,
swallow flowers, swallow

fields, drop by drop, each stem
a pump. Rose to rose to rose to
rose, all summer

 gone, pistil &

petal. We move
still faster, fields grow

constant, inside
the color of heat. Clinging we
pull our bodies

across a chain of bodies, become

the chain, climb nothing,
always
up, toward suns, line them up

inside us, a flower taken whole,

a field built inside. It rises.
Each blade, each sun.

Gregory Orr

BE-ALL

(for Stanley)

The insect clings
to the green
stalk, sucks
its sap,
holds to the world
because it knows
the world is whole and holy—the be-all
and the end-all
of it.

      But me—
I feel I'm ghost
and gristle
both.
      My sickness
is to think
there's something
out there called
the Infinite—

a place where
all my longing
will become *belong*.

Tess Gallagher

BEHAVE

Central word of my childhood.
A father's plea that could turn
command, then verge on threat: *behave,*
I want you to behave now.
This bright morning promises a cathedral
when a chapel will do to praise this word, tender
enough over years to slice the distance
into the two halves of any question—
what we might have done and what we came
to do. To question such authority meant
a pirouette of backward glances or intention

like a freight train finding and loading up
its reasons. *If you don't behave,* he'd say,
desperation mounting for the din of household
to let him have, after the day's labor, some
riverbank-moment where stillness
could come, could eddy and release him back
into his "far away"—that place we could sense him
wanting to get to
like a drowning man whose life seems the far shore
when it is a breath at the lip
of a watery precipice

under him. Roethke, my other long gone father,
paraphrasing Marianne Moore
to tell us: "*Once we feel deeply*
we begin to behave."

Alan Dugan

JEWELS OF INDOOR GLASS

The broken glass on the stairs
shines in the electric light.
Whoever dropped the beer
was anti-social or too drunk
to sweep it up himself.
So the beauty goes, ground
under heel but shining, it
and the deposit lost. But
by the janitor's broom
it is still sharp enough
for dogs' feet, babies' hands,
and eyes pierced by its lights,
that he should curse the fool
and I should try to praise
the pieces of harmony.

Alan Dugan

THE DARK TOWER

*After George Gordon, Lord
Byron, the revolutionary
democrat and lover of
Greece, 1788-1824.*

The swamp around the tower was alive
with animals and was an animal itself.
Everybody looked at everybody; things
felt out things until it was Resolved:
Who is the strongest. Then the animals
attacked, ran, or fawned; the swamp
held up its tracks or let them drop.
The old black keep which I approached
past fawning animals on solid bog
was no more awful than a broken tooth
except for the man who has it. I knocked
to test his nerve and stake my claim
to what is mine by nature, his by name.

Alan Dugan

ON LOOKING FOR MODELS

The trees in time
have something else to do
besides their treeing. What is it.
I'm a starving to death
man myself, and thirsty, thirsty
by their fountains but I cannot drink
their mud and sunlight to be whole.
I do not understand these presences
that drink for months
in the dirt, eat light,
and then fast dry in the cold;
they stand it out somehow,
and how, the Botanists will tell me.
It is the "something else" that bothers
me, so I often go back to the forests.

Contributors' Notes

Only the most recent and forthcoming publications are listed.

Dannie Abse, the Welsh poet, *Be Seated Thou*, Sheep Meadow Press, 2000.

Elise Asher, *Night Train*, Sheep Meadow Press, 2001. She is also known as Mrs. Stanley Kunitz.

Peter Balakian, *June-Tree, New and Selected Poems*, Harper Collins, 2001.

Stephen Berg, *Footnotes to an Unfinished Poem*, Orchises Press, 2001.

Robert Bly, *The Night Abraham Called to the Stars*, Harper Collins, 2001. He won the 1968 National Book Award.

Bodhan Boychuck, the Ukrainian poet, *Memories of Love*, Sheep Meadow Press, 1989.

Lucille Clifton, *Blessing the Boats: New and Selected Poems 1988-2000*, BOA Editions, Ltd., 2000. She won the 2000 National Book Award.

Peter Davison, *Breathing Room: New Poems*, Alfred A. Knopf, 2000.

Tory Dent, *HIV, Mon Amour*, Sheep Meadow Press, 1999. She won the 1999 James Laughlin Award.

Diana Der-Hovanessian, *Any Day Now*, Sheep Meadow Press, 1999.

Alan Dugan, forthcoming *Poems Seven: New and Selected Poems*, Seven Stories Press, 2001. He won the 1962 Pulitzer Prize and the 1962 National Book Award

Allison Funk, forthcoming *Heart's-Ease*, Sheep Meadow Press, 2002.

Nick Flynn, *Some Ether*, Graywolf Press, 2000. He won the 2000 James Laughlin Award.

Tess Gallagher, *Soul Barnacles*, University of Michigan Press, 2000.

Forrest Gander, *Torn Awake*, New Directions, 2001.

Louise Glück, *The Seven Ages*, Ecco, 2001. She won the 1985 Critics Circle Award and the 1993 Pulitzer Prize.

Arthur Gregor, forthcoming *That Other Side of Things*, Sheep Meadow Press, 2001.

Seamus Heaney, *Electric Light*, Farrar, Straus & Giroux, 2001. He received the 1995 Nobel Prize in Literature.

Shirley Kaufman, *Roots in the Air: New and Selected Poems*, Copper Canyon Press, 1996.

Galway Kinnell, *New and Selected Poems*, Houghton Mifflin Co., 2000. He won the 1983 Pulitzer Prize and the 1983 National Book Award.

Carolyn Kizer, *Cool Calm & Collected*, Copper Canyon Press, 2001. She won the 1985 Pulitzer Prize.

Kenneth Koch, *New Addresses*, Alfred A. Knopf, 2000. He won the 1995 Bollingen Prize.

Yusef Komunyakaa, *Pleasure Dome: New & Collected Poems, 1975-1999*, Wesleyan University Press, 2001. He won the 1994 Pulitzer Prize and the 2001 Ruth Lilly Prize.

Maxine Kumin, *The Long Marriage*, W.W. Norton, 2001. She won the 1973 Pulitzer Prize and the 1999 Ruth Lilly Prize.

Anne Marie Macari, *Ivory Cradle*, Copper Canyon Press, 2000.

Cleopatra Mathis, *What to Tip the Boatman?*, Sheep Meadow Press, 2001.

Gail Mazur, *They Can't Take That Away From Me*, University of Chicago Press, 2001.

W. S. Merwin, *The Pupil*, Alfred A. Knopf, 2001. He won the 1971 Pulitzer Prize, the 1979 Bollingen Prize and the 1998 Ruth Lilly Prize.

Christopher Middleton, *The Word Pavilion and Selected Poems*, Sheep Meadow Press, 2001.

Susan Mitchell, *Erotikon*, Harper Collins, 2001.

Stanley Moss, forthcoming *A History of Color and Other Poems, New and Selected*, Seven Stories Press 2002.

Paul Muldoon, *Poems: 1968-1998*, Farrar, Straus & Giroux, 2001. He is Professor at Princeton University and the University of Oxford.

Sharon Olds, *Blood Tin Straw*, Alfred A. Knopf, 1999. She won the 1984 Critics Circle Award.

Mary Oliver, *The Leaf and the Cloud, A Poem*, Da Capo Press, 2001. She won the 1984 Pulitzer Prize and the 1992 National Book Award.

Gregory Orr, *Orpheus and Eurydice*, Copper Canyon Press, 2000.

Stanley Plumly, *Now That My Father Lies Down Beside Me: New and Selected Poems, 1970-2000*, Ecco, 2000.

Alberto Ríos, forthcoming *The Smallest Muscle in the Human Body*, Copper Canyon Press, 2002.

Mark Rudman, *Provoked in Venice*, Wesleyan University Press, 1999. He won the 1994 Critics Circle Award.

Michael Ryan, *A Difficult Grace: On Poets, Poetry, and Writing*, University of Georgia Press, 2000.

Grace Schulman, *The Paintings of Our Lives*, Houghton Mifflin Co., 2001.

Hugh Seidman, *Selected Poems: 1965-1995*, Miami University Press, 1995.

Bruce Smith, *The Other Lover*, University of Chicago Press, 2000.

Gerald Stern, *American Sonnets*, W.W. Norton, 2000. He won the 1998 National Book Award.

Reetika Vazirani, forthcoming *World Hotel*, Copper Canyon Press 2002.

Joshua Weiner, *The World's Room*, University of Chicago Press, 2001.

Richard Wilbur, *Mayflies*, Harcourt Inc., 2000. He won the 1957 National Book Award, the 1971 Bollingen Prize and the 1989 Pulitzer Prize.

OTHER TITLES FROM SHEEP MEADOW

Stanley Kunitz
Interviews and Encounters

Paul Celan
Fathomsuns and Benighted
Collected Prose
Correspondence: Nelly Sachs and Paul Celan

Yehuda Amichai
Poems of Jerusalem and Love Poems
The Great Tranquillity
Travels
The Early Books of Yehuda Amichai

F.T. Prince
Selected Poems and Other Writings
Collected Poems
Walks in Rome
The Yüan Chên Variations

Umberto Saba
Songbook
History and Chronicle of the Songbook
Stories and Recollections

Fernando Pessoa
The Book of Disquietude
The Keeper of Sheep

Tory Dent
HIV, Mon Amour

Cleopatra Mathis
What To Tip The Boatman?

Hans Magnus Enzensberger
Lighter Than Air
Kiosk
Selected Poems

Dannie Abse
Be Seated Thou

Tomas Venclova
Forms of Hope

Aharon Shabtai
Love and Selected Poems

Yona Wallach
Wild Light

Rebecca Seiferle
The Music We Dance To
The Ripped-Out Seam

Christopher Middleton
The Word Pavilion and Selected Poems
Intimate Chronicles
The Balcony Tree

John Peck
A·R·G·V·R·A
Poems and Translations of Hĭ-Lö

César Vallejo
Trilce

Mary Kinzie
Summers of Vietnam

David Ignatow
Notebooks

SWEET
CHARLOTTE'S
seventh mistake

CORI CROOKS

SEAL PRESS

SWEET CHARLOTTE'S SEVENTH MISTAKE

Published by
Seal Press
A Member of the Perseus Books Group
1700 Fourth Street
Berkeley, CA 94710

Library of Congress Cataloging-in-Publication Data

Crooks, Cori.
  Sweet Charlotte's seventh mistake / by Cori Crooks.
    p. cm.
  ISBN-13: 978-1-58005-249-8
  ISBN-10: 1-58005-249-5
  1. Crooks, Cori—Family. 2. Problem families—United States. I.
Title.
  CT275.C887455 A3 2008
  973.91092—dc22
  [B]

                              2008020990

Cover and Interior design by Domini Dragoone
Printed in Thailand by Imago
Distributed by Publishers Group West

For Porter
and Miles Ray

Contents

The Letter................................... 8

The Stamp 10

We, the Living 14

Prayers 18

Beach Blanket Bingo.................... 20

Apple Season 22

1974, Winter............................... 24

Grannyphone?............................. 28

1975, Summer PART I 30

A.K.A. Mommy 35

Haiku for Paterfamilias.................. 36

1975, Summer PART 2 38

Shackles and Bluebells................... 40

Failing Basic Math 42

Mama....................................... 46

My First Lie............................... 50

Girl with Half an Eyebrow............... 52

Gravidity 60

Detached 64

Baby #1 66

Alcatraz 68

Some of What He Left Me 70

No Hard Hat 74

Shoe Lottery 76

My Darling Clementine 78

Sleepwalking 82

Baby and the Bathwater 86

Baby #2 88

2 Years, a Couch, and a Birthday 90

Owls in Sand 94

Driving Lessons 98

The Abortion 102

Word Problems 104

Movie House 106

Babies #3 & #4 108

The Science Fair Lie 110

My Strange Nose 114

Hanoi Jane vs. My Mom 118

The Other Grandmother 120

Pennies from Heaven 124

The Rules 128

Baby #5 132

Promenade Girl 134

Reunion PART 1 138

Reunion PART 2 143

A Nominative Case 146

I Hate Your Answering Machine 148

Rule #2: The VW Bug 150

Baby #6 156

Declining the Crown 158

Girl Trouble 1 164

Love, Soft as an Easy Chair 166

Girl Trouble 2 168

Altamont 172

Girl Trouble 3 176

The Other Brothers 180

Dear Diary 184

Girl Trouble 4 186

Taking the Test 190

Baby #7 192

4 and 20 Blackbirds 194

The Results 198

Born 201

Acknowledgments 204

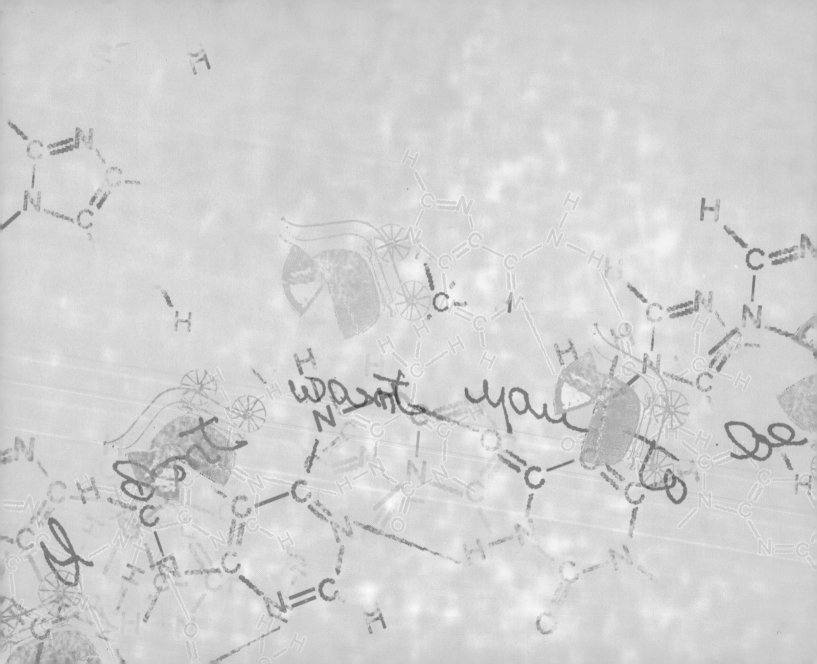

I don't want you to be like me.

7

a good child will pay honor
to their Mother and Father

THE LETTER

7/22/04

Dear David H. Schnabel,

I am sure that you remember me,

CeAnne's daughter Cori—we have met many times and I have
very fond memories of your visits.

I hope this letter finds you well,
and that life has been good for you.

I have tried throughout the last 13 years to find you, but sadly I was unable.
I think it's pretty incredible that I have now—after all this time.

I am very sorry to share with you that my
Mom passed away on January 23, 1991.

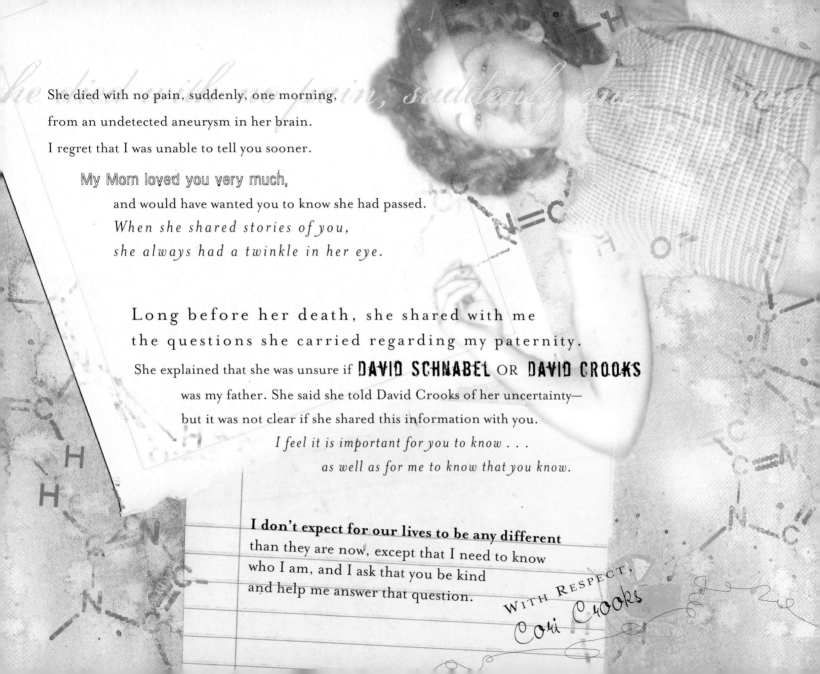

She died with no pain, suddenly, one morning,

from an undetected aneurysm in her brain.

I regret that I was unable to tell you sooner.

My Mom loved you very much,

and would have wanted you to know she had passed.
When she shared stories of you,
she always had a twinkle in her eye.

Long before her death, she shared with me
the questions she carried regarding my paternity.

She explained that she was unsure if **DAVID SCHNABEL** OR **DAVID CROOKS**

was my father. She said she told David Crooks of her uncertainty—

but it was not clear if she shared this information with you.

I feel it is important for you to know . . .

as well as for me to know that you know.

I don't expect for our lives to be any different
than they are now, except that I need to know
who I am, and I ask that you be kind
and help me answer that question.

WITH RESPECT,
Cori Crooks

THE STAMP

I think hope was invented by the post office.

It was some sort of made-up slogan, complete with emotional attachment, created to sell stamps back before Elvis came along.

But not the stamps with the easy sticker backing . . . no.
I'm talking about those old-fashioned stamps, the ones you had to lick.
The ones that left a bad taste in your mouth.

I sent the letter. I wrote it when I finally knew where he was.
I had tried different searches every few years after my Mom died.
I thought he worked on a farm, so I called farms. I thought he lived near Yosemite, so I checked phone books and property records of outlying towns.

Every few years I'd check
    and recheck what I'd checked before—
        but I had no idea how to spell his name.

ENDLESS
COMBINATIONS.

Smabble
SNOBLE
SCHNOBEL

Then came the day I spelled it right. Schnabel, David Hans Schnabel,
and I found him. And like I said, when I found him I wrote the letter—
but there was this second, *this frozen second,*
when the letter fell from my fingertips and
into the mailbox. In that second, I could
have sworn that I could taste a
fake mint flavor.

You see, I have a father.
He's pretty great. He's attractive and kind, and has always cared for me.
The only problem is, he lives in a photo album.
He died when I was a baby.

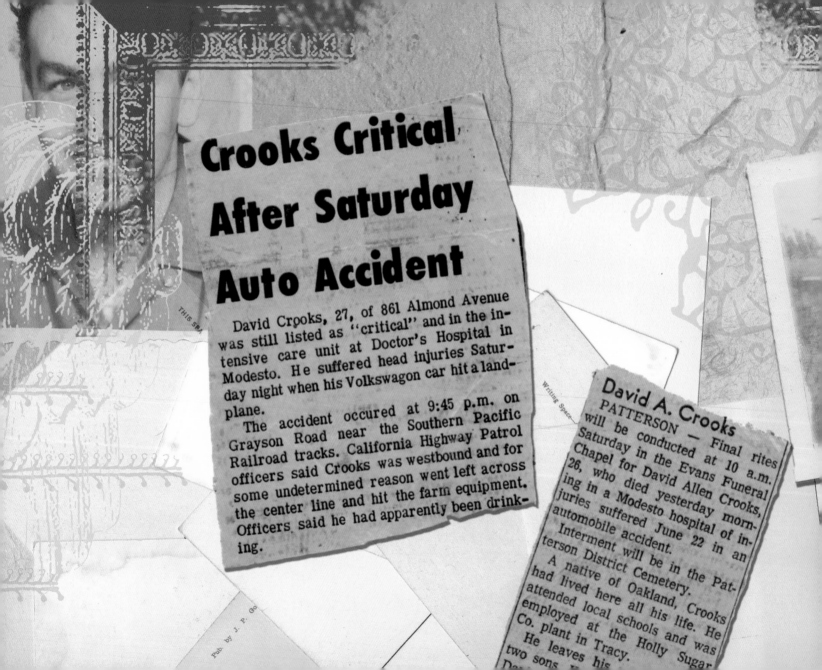

Crooks Critical After Saturday Auto Accident

David Crooks, 27, of 861 Almond Avenue was still listed as "critical" and in the intensive care unit at Doctor's Hospital in Modesto. He suffered head injuries Saturday night when his Volkswagon car hit a land-plane.

The accident occured at 9:45 p.m. on Grayson Road near the Southern Pacific Railroad tracks. California Highway Patrol officers said Crooks was westbound and for some undetermined reason went left across the center line and hit the farm equipment. Officers said he had apparently been drink-ing.

David A. Crooks

PATTERSON — Final rites will be conducted at 10 a.m. Saturday in the Evans Funeral Chapel for David Allen Crooks, 26, who died yesterday morning in a Modesto hospital of injuries suffered June 22 in an automobile accident.

Interment will be in the Patterson District Cemetery.

A native of Oakland, Crooks had lived here all his life. He attended local schools and was employed at the Holly Sugar Co. plant in Tracy.

He leaves his two sons

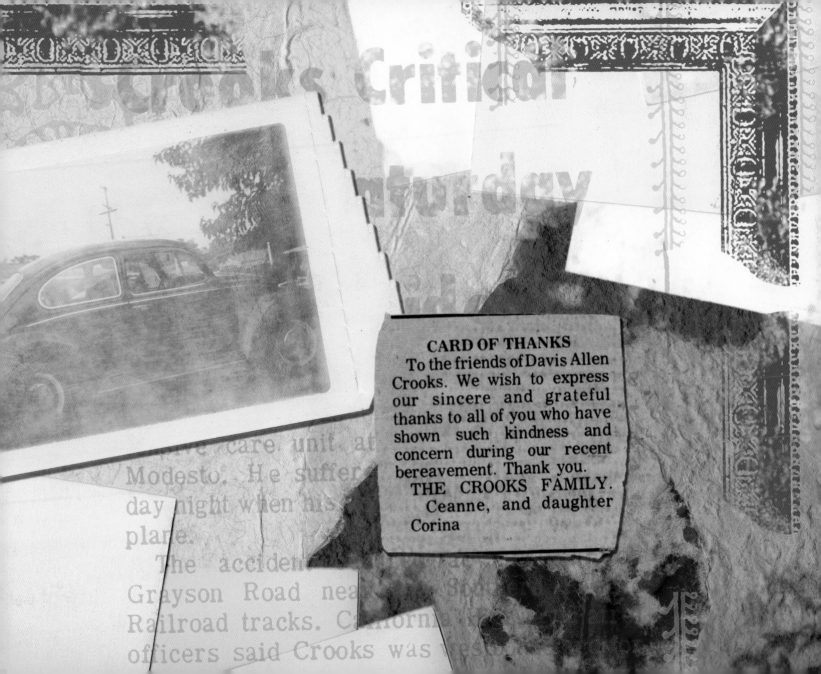

CARD OF THANKS
To the friends of Davis Allen Crooks. We wish to express our sincere and grateful thanks to all of you who have shown such kindness and concern during our recent bereavement. Thank you.
THE CROOKS FAMILY.
Ceanne, and daughter Corina

...ve care unit at Modesto. He suffer... day night when his... plane.

The acciden... Grayson Road nea... S... Railroad tracks. California... officers said Crooks was...

We, the Living...

David Crooks died in the summer of 1970.

I was 11 months old. He died July 10, eleven days before my first birthday. *I practically grew up at his gravesite.*

My Mom, CeAnne, would say,
"I always know if I'm doing
good or bad when I come here."

On the way to visit,
we would stop at the flower shop
in the village center of Patterson.

A sweet Portuguese man would give

us flowers even when my Mom

couldn't pay him.

At the cemetery, she would sit against
the front end of our station wagon,
smoking Lucky Strike cigarettes.

She held her cigarette between
her index and middle fingers,
extended out in front of her.

Her view of the world always had a tail of smoke attached.

NON-FILTERED.

I would talk to my father,
the knees of my pants soaked with
grass water. I'd dig up little rocks
and place them atop his headstone.
I'd bury little presents under the soil.
Usually my earrings.

Then I would walk back to Mom and the car,
being very careful not to step on anyone's grave.

My Grandpa Porter
was buried to the right
of my Dad. He passed
away a year or two after him.

My Mom always said,
"That empty space on the
other side of your Dad's is
meant for you."

This is a true day by day
story of a girl without a brain
and with even less sence.

Every love I set I loose.

CARD OF THANKS
To the friends of Davis Alle
expre
gratef
who ha
ess
rece
you.
FAMIL
daught

APR

PRAYERS

Now I lay me down to sleep,
I pray the Lord my soul to keep.
If I should die before I wake,
I pray the Lord my soul to take.
God bless Greg, Peter, Marsha, Jan,
Bobby, Cindy, Dennis, and Ronnie.

When I was 5, I didn't know the totality of what I was saying.

I didn't go to church, let alone understand that I was something other than my *Mother's daughter,* or the name that I thought ended that list.

I recited the prayer as I was taught. I was told it would make me good.
I added those names secretly, and I faithfully said those names every night.

There was something in me that drew me to them.
I felt they belonged to me. They were "mines."
They were my brothers and they were my sisters.

I don't really know when it was—that bright moment when I understood that the something I was part of was a big big mess. None of us had the same two parents, save the twins. Some of us didn't know our fathers, and those that did know their fathers—didn't. Most of us didn't even know each other—except through stories, or pictures, or in my case, lists.

. . . I'd find out later that my list was a bit screwed up.

Possible Sibling Count: Ten.

Mom's kids

GREG .... 3/58 (raised by father)

PETER .... 5/59 (father unknown, raised in foster care)

MARSHA .... 4/60 (raised in foster care)

JAN .... 4/60 (raised in foster care, dead)

BOBBY .... 11/62 (lived on and off w/Mom, kicked out by 15)

CINDY .... 1/65 (lived on and off w/Mom, father unknown)

(ME, DEFINITELY) .... 7/69 (lived on and off w/Mom, terribly confused about who father really is)

David Crooks's kids

DENNIS .... DOB? 40 yrs? (raised by mother)

RONNIE .... DOB? 38 yrs? (raised by mother)

(I fit here, or so I thought)

David Schnabel's kids

KIMMY .... DOB? 36 yrs?

(me, possibly—it's all so strange)

CARLA .... DOB? 33 yrs? (A younger sister? Wow.)

BEACH BLANKET BINGO

My mother's figure was not at all affected by
6 pregnancies/7 births.

In 1970 she gave up the snake,
and had retired from what she called
exotic dancing by the time I was a toddler.

For years to come I would play dress up in her
wigs, boots, and sequined bras.

She stored her past in 3 patent leather hatboxes. They zipped up like bowling ball bags.

My Mom said she was in *Beach Blanket Bingo*,
but her part got cut. She said Annette Funicello was a real bitch.

I think I'm pregnant again.

APPLE SEASON

1/4 Irish/
American Indian Princess
OR RUSSIAN?
HUNGARIAN?
German?
Jewess?

august 8, 2004

The question stands,
while I sit with an apple blossom
crown on my lap.

David Hans Schnabel finally
wrote back and drew eyes in the
O's of my name on the envelope.

David Hans Schnabel grieved
for my mother 13 years late.

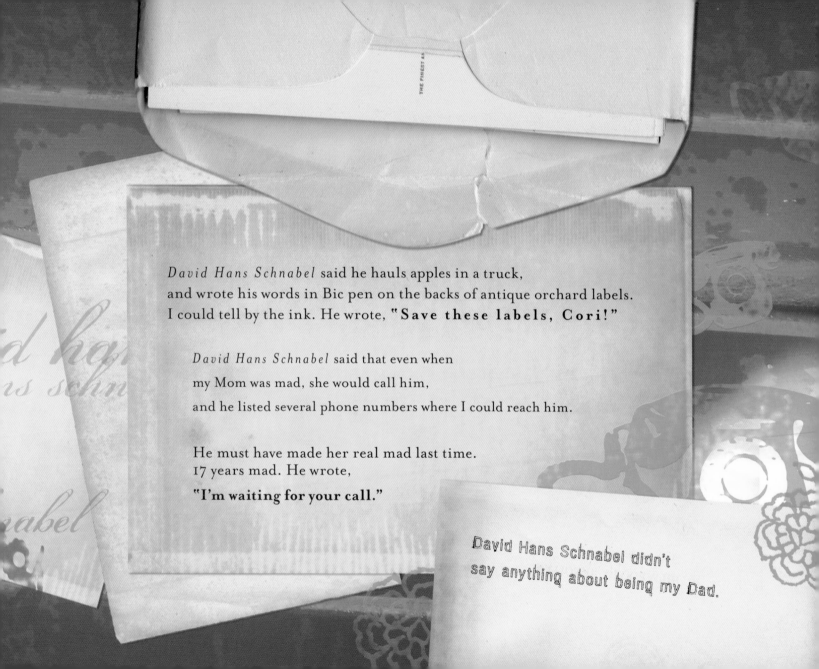

David Hans Schnabel said he hauls apples in a truck,
and wrote his words in Bic pen on the backs of antique orchard labels.
I could tell by the ink. He wrote, **"Save these labels, Cori!"**

David Hans Schnabel said that even when

my Mom was mad, she would call him,

and he listed several phone numbers where I could reach him.

He must have made her real mad last time.
17 years mad. He wrote,

"I'm waiting for your call."

David Hans Schnabel didn't
say anything about being my Dad.

1974, WINTER

I believe I was just 5 years old during the winter of 1974. Mom sat us down and told us what radiation treatments were.

She was dying.

This would be our last Christmas together.

Bobby would get sent out to the Dad he'd never met, in Pennsylvania.

Cindy would go live with Great-Grandma.

Naturally, the twins and Peter would stay with their foster family. They had been there since they were real little, but that was rarely mentioned.

Mom said she didn't know where our oldest brother, Greg, was. She said his family was rich and took Greg away from her after she gave birth. She never said where I was supposed to go.

For now, we 4 needed to stick close together.

We were all she had left. We needed to make this the best Christmas ever, she said.

There were so many things she needed to teach us.

I would do as Cindy said,

and stop at the corner to knock on the knot

of the grand old oak while walking home from school.

It was a neighborhood tradition.

Cindy said an owl lived in there. MR. OWL.

He got real lonely and needed to know that people cared.

I knocked every day. *He was never home.*

This time, my mother was waiting for me at that corner.

She said she had a special surprise for me. She made me promise

never to tell. It might make Bobby and Cindy feel sad.

She handed me my UMBRELLA and said, "You forgot this."

I grabbed her hand and took her to the oak.

She said she thought it might be a weeping willow.

despite th

We spent that day on Fisherman's Wharf.

We ate clam chowder out of sourdough bowls.
We stood outside of Ripley's Believe It or Not! and stared at
the fingernails on the statue of a man made from human parts.
We kept my **umbrella** *closed and walked in the rain.*

That night my mother reclined on the couch, drinking slow

sips of her 7UP. She refused any food her boyfriend brought.

"Radiation sickness," she told him. "The treatments

lasted all day. You don't remember, do you?"

The phone rang. She winked at me.

She answered with a weak voice.

My mother faked cancer twice in her life.
Both times, I was the only one who knew the truth.

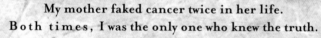

It was the best Christmas
I remember.

Letters to the editor

A beautiful Christmas, despite the misfortunes

EDITOR: Every time I pick up a newspaper lately it's full of all the bad, unhappy, horrible things that people are doing and saying, and very seldom (if at all) the kindness and caring that is still here. I'd like to share my happiness this Christmas season with all of the Bay Area.

You see, my husband has been off work for three months, and, as I am undergoing treatments for cancer, I am unable to work. We are not eligible for aid because we get $250 a month Social Security for my three children.

About two weeks ago what money and groceries we had were running out, and it looked to be a very bleak and sad Christmas for us. We couldn't even feed the kids, let alone buy any presents for them.

But thanks to our neighbors, my daughter's kindergarten teacher and school nurse, we truly had a beautiful old-fashioned Christmas. In fact, much better than we would have had if we had been working.

Thanks to the many people who know us, we had a beautiful Christmas tree and more presents than I ever dreamed possible. There was a turkey in the oven, the trimmings in the icebox, and our cupboards were full. Clothes, money, toys, food, all have taught me and mine that Christmas isn't all commercialized. The love and giving is still here and will shine brightly in the eyes of my children.

I am not only grateful, but amazed, because I was one of those who thought people didn't care. But they do care, and the biggest and best present of all is the love that I have seen.

All the money in the world couldn't repay each person for what we have learned this year!

C. HENDRYX
Hayward

The Daily Review   Hayward, Calif.
Tuesday, December 31, 1974

GRANNYPHONE?

I've never liked telephones.

Maybe it's that awkward feeling in the small talk
that comes before the something that you've got
to say. No one calls just to call—
there is always something.

Being the someone who has the something this time,
and a big something indeed,
makes me *hate* the phone even more.

"Hi, yeah—life's funny, isn't it? Ha ha, yeah—
I might be your kid! **Wanna take a test?"**

David Hans Schnabel wrote out 3 phone numbers in his letter, but he wasn't too clear on the who and the where. Maybe he was nervous. I've tried 2. One seemed to go to a beeper, the other was picked up by an old lady. She must be his Mom.

Ring, *ring* · · ·
ring, ring · · ·
ring, ring · · ·
ri · · ·   Pause.

"Hello?" *(old, frail crackle)*

"Hi. Can I speak to David?"

(click)

"Hello? . . . Hello?"

(dial tone)

I guess she doesn't like phones either.

1975, SUMMER PART 1

Mom had been gone for 9 days.

Each day her boyfriend, whom she referred to as
her husband, sat down quietly on the couch and
stared at his hands. He wouldn't look at me when
I spoke to him. Janet whispered,
>*"It's because you look like Mom."*

Everything living became lifeless.
Our dogs didn't bark.
No breeze came in through the back.
Hush and still. Cindy and Bobby stayed in their rooms.
Shh and dumb.

The fake husband

continued his silent sit,

there on his quiet couch.

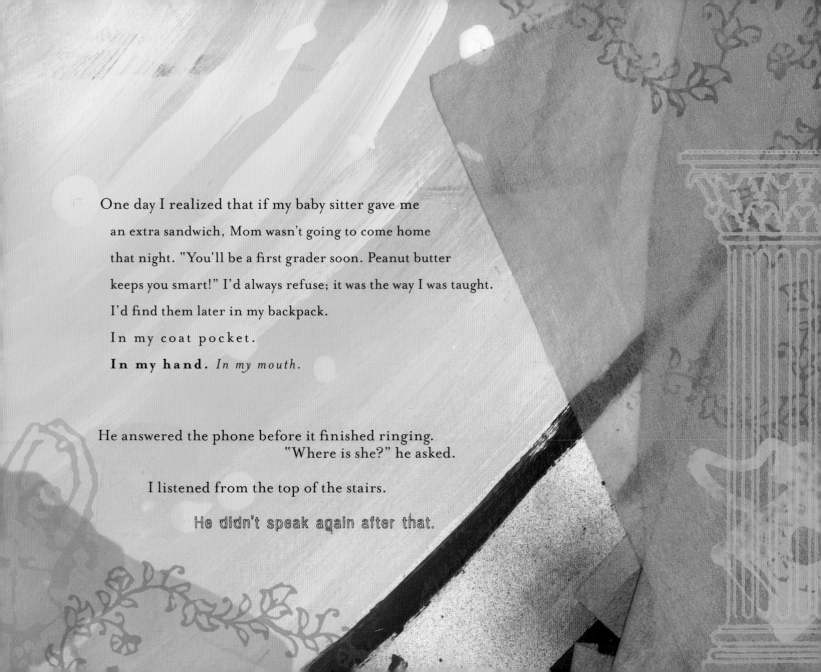

One day I realized that if my baby sitter gave me
an extra sandwich, Mom wasn't going to come home
that night. "You'll be a first grader soon. Peanut butter
keeps you smart!" I'd always refuse; it was the way I was taught.
I'd find them later in my backpack.
In my coat pocket.
In my hand. *In my mouth.*

He answered the phone before it finished ringing.
                    "Where is she?" he asked.

I listened from the top of the stairs.

        He didn't speak again after that.

I closed my eyes
and went out to the orchard on Grayson Road.
I found my Dad picking peaches.

He climbed down from his ladder

and handed me a perfect fruit.

Its color blended into my skin.

I couldn't see my fingers against its pink flesh.

I told him that the wind had stopped blowing.

I told him that my Mom was lost again.

I asked him to bring her back.

I cried in the arms of a ghost.

I slept with a peach pit deep in my hold.

"Cori, Cori, wake up, honey," the fake husband
whispered through the smell of alcohol and tobacco.

I rubbed my eyes. A small box was waiting in his hand.
"I got this for you, sunshine. It's a ring."

A gold-plated band twisted into 2 leaves

that held a plastic mother-of-pearl cabochon.

The prettiest ring I had ever seen.

The letter **C** was carved on the top.

"If you ever need me,
I want you to put this ring in an envelope and mail it to me.
No matter where I'm at, I'll come and get you," he said.
I nodded.

He tucked the covers in and walked out
of my room. Cindy snuck in behind him,
pointed to the window,
and whispered, "Look! Mom's home!"

A.K.A. Mommy

When my Mom died, her seventh
and final husband went to the social
security office to report her death. . . .
They didn't know who
he was talking about.

Charlotte Anne Luster
Charlotte Anne Laird
Charlotte Luster Johnson
CAL
Darla Kell
Kelly Kell
Charlotte Trapp
Charlotte McDonald
Charlotte A. Brimberry
D. CeAnne Brimberry
D. CeAnne Crooks
Darla C. Higgs
D. CeAnne Hendryx
CeAnna Hendryx
CeAnna Stein

He asked me to make a list of names
my mother went by when she was alive.

I did the best I could.

HAIKU FOR THE PATERFAMILIAS

She made the phone call.
Fingers fall with each ring–still,
Mr. Owl's not home.

Toward the end of August, I started to think that

David Hans Schnabel might have blown me off.

I reminded myself that this was a man who had been
involved with MY MOTHER.

The odds of him being a stand-up sorta guy were
PRETTY SLIM.

No matter how often I tried,
I couldn't get ahold of him, and I didn't understand
why he didn't just call me.

I found myself reaching for something
to ease an impending letdown.

His letter was full of misspelled words.
Yeah, but then, I'm a pretty bad speller myself.

He sent me 3 phone numbers—
he doesn't seem to have his own phone.
Yeah, but maybe he just wanted to be sure I could
reach him. He does drive trucks for a living, after all.

His writing, mixed with drawings,

reminded me of the letters my

brother Bobby would send from prison.

His writing reminded me of jailhouse letters.

Yeah.
It looked like a jailhouse letter.
It did.

1975, SUMMER PART 2

Mom is home.

She was leaning into the driver's window of a
green Cadillac that was parked in our driveway.

The white pleather roof matched her crocheted pantsuit,
the one she wore when she wanted to look pretty.

The one she ruined when she fell, wasted, from that same
car, after another long disappearance, a year or so later.

She was talking to someone. Cindy said it was Larry,
the twins' daddy, back in the picture. They began kissing.
He handed her something. She stood up and placed that
something in her bra, still talking.

The car pulled away, leaving her glowing
in the bright moonlight.

*When this book is
full I want to go back
through and find out
if I've grown up and
or maybe even gotten
worse*

CeAnne

She looked up to the bedroom
window, and for a moment
she caught my eye.

Thank you, Daddy.

I remember him yelling.
I remember her screaming.
I remember running down the
stairs and seeing his gentle hands
around her neck, squeezing.

No, Mommy, no.

Bobby took the stairs by twos,

pushing through me and our sister.

Bobby jumped on his back

and he hit and hit.

Over and over again,

until those silent hands fell from our

mother's neck,

until he was no longer a boy—

and long after the fake husband left,

Bobby hit and hit at the still air,

until he was a broken man.

Puzzles with missing pieces get thrown away.

That summer passed in 9 lost days
and blew behind me somehow.
Again, I found myself at my Dad's grave,
and I left the ring with him.

SHACKLES AND BLUEBELLS

There is a charm bracelet floating around the wrist
of my great-grandmother's house.

On that charm bracelet hang 7 silver cameos—

they catch the light and reflect

unfamiliar faces against the skin of her quiet hallway.

Engraved on those dangling heads

are the names and birth dates of forgotten babies,

who cry their buried stories

and are hushed by the lullaby of charm against chain. . . .

She opens her arms wide and peers out from
her worried windows,

calling for the 7 children
who had no home.

FAILING BASIC MATH

I've always been the baby of what there was and what there wasn't of my family.

I was my Mom's baby.

David Crooks called me his baby.

David Schnabel *must have known* that I might be his.

If I am the daughter of DAVID CROOKS, who was the youngest son of 5 children . . .

I am the youngest of **7** from my Mom, and the youngest of **3** from my Dad. *In total . . . the youngest of* **10**.

There are 7 wonders of the world.
          Cats have 9 lives.
There are 12 steps in most recovery programs.

If I am the daughter of DAVID SCHNABEL,

sibling count unknown...

I am the youngest of 7 from my Mom, who is the eldest of 3,

          but raised by her grandmother, whom she called Mom,

making her the baby of 5...

          and I am the second eldest of 3 from you know who,

          who is still a who. Totaling *10* again.

Some people follow the 10 Commandments.
          3 is a magic number, and I've always been the baby.
7 brides for 7 brothers, and I could be her big sister.

**You have only one life to live.
But I find myself living two.**

I spoke to her.
Carla, his baby daughter.

I called the last phone number
he gave me in that letter.

She picked up right away,
and she didn't sound anything like a SISTER.

She doesn't know me.
She took my name and number
and asked who I was.

"Your Dad knew my Mom," subtracting.

She asked me to hold.
I heard her addressing the voices of children/nieces/nephews/strangers?

"Who are you?" she asked with a tone.

I didn't know what to say.

Yeah . . . who am I?

"Your Dad was a friend of my family," I added.

MAMA

I heard that methamphetamine
got its nickname, crank,
Because Hells Angels would hide
their stash in the crankshaft
of their motorcycles.

That's what Mom said they did back then.

Mom said a lot of things about "back then"—a lot of things that I've
spent my life cutting and dividing, looking for the truth of her.

I read her old diaries. *Diaries that are closer to empty than to full.*
Occasional days are filled in. Sometimes there are three days in a row,
maybe a week. Sometimes I see a mirror of who she might have been.
What might have made her do the things she did.

1966

"This is a true day-by-day story of a girl
without a brain and with even less sense.
Every love I get I lose because I'm too stupid
to be able to do or say the right things."

−CEANNE

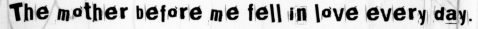

The mother before me fell in love every day.

She defined herself by the love of a man. *Well, many men.*

These men took precedence over her children.
She rarely mentions any of us in her diaries. She doesn't even circle our birth dates.
When she wrote these entries, **6** of us had already been born.

(I didn't come along until '69.)

may 21, 1966
"My birthday. Johnny gave me the most beautiful
engagement rings. We are afraid to tell his folks.
I got very drunk and don't remember much else."

july 2, 1966

"I left Johnny at the Laundromat.

I went back home and got my check,

moved to 4th and Maine with Scott,

he's on Ed's ship. He took me

to see fireworks on the pike."

august 7, 1966
Started going with Matt.
He sure is sharp!
Candy fixed us up at her birthday party."

MAY 21 My birthday

Johnny gave me the most
beautiful engagement rings
We are afraid to tell his
folks. I got very drunk &
don't remember much else

The names she does mention, besides the men's,
are not our names. They are other names.

Uppers. **CROSSTOPS**. Yellowjackets. Beans.

Pills of dextroamphetamine and methamphetamine,
legally manufactured in the 1950s and readily available for dieting,
depression, and addiction. Mother's Little Helpers,

even for the world's most reluctant mother.

I wonder if that's where she got started.

october 8, 1966
"Picked up pills and spent the day
washing and *cleaning* the kitchen floor.

Went riding with George and some of his friends.

Matt and I felt out of place. They were all older people
and not really bike riders. Just grandpas going through

their second childhood.

We went to Santa Monica and it would have
been fun if we had been alone. Both of us had
a hard time going to sleep,

TOO MANY PILLS."

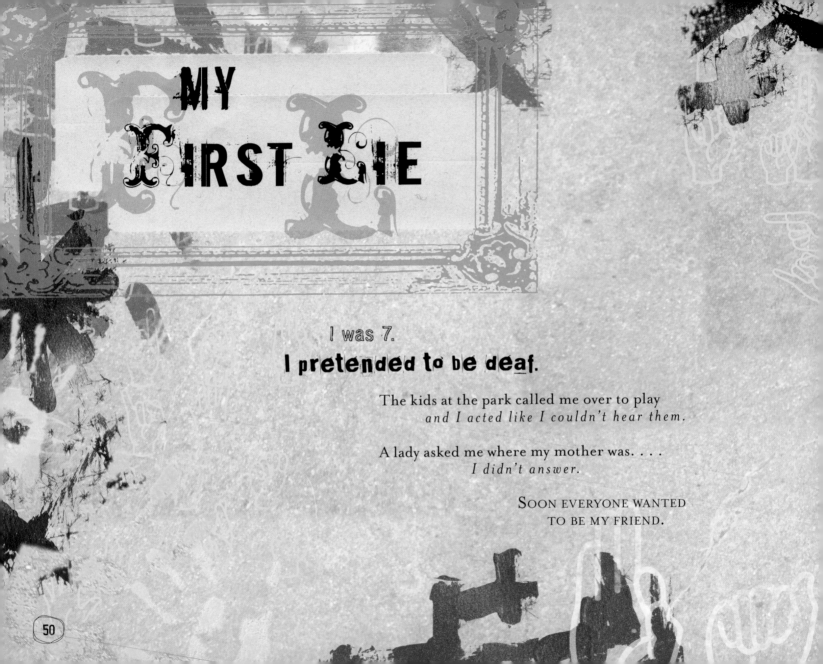

MY FIRST LIE

I was 7.

I pretended to be deaf.

The kids at the park called me over to play
and I acted like I couldn't hear them.

A lady asked me where my mother was. . . .
I didn't answer.

SOON EVERYONE WANTED
TO BE MY FRIEND.

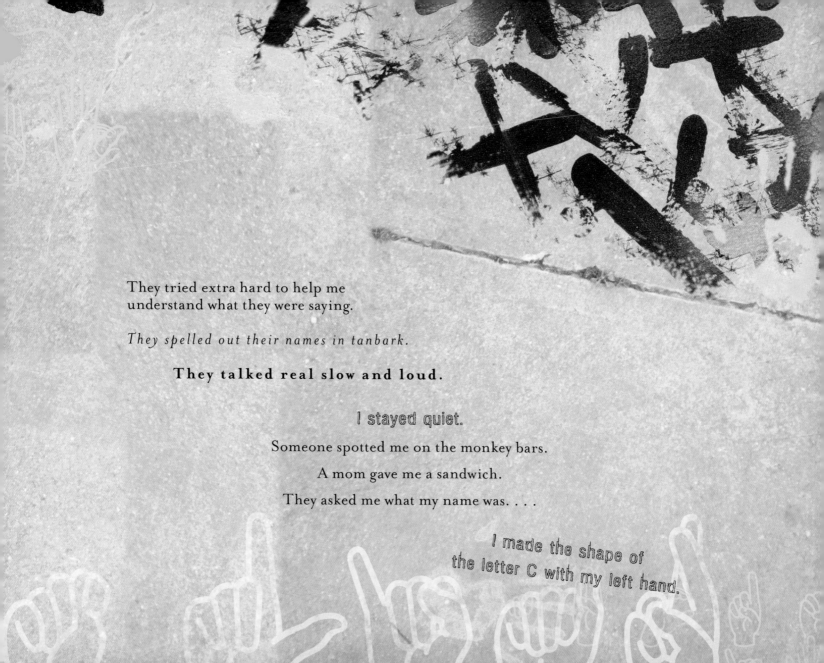

They tried extra hard to help me
understand what they were saying.

They spelled out their names in tanbark.

They talked real slow and loud.

I stayed quiet.

Someone spotted me on the monkey bars.

A mom gave me a sandwich.

They asked me what my name was. . . .

I made the shape of
the letter C with my left hand.

THE GIRL WITH
HALF AN EYEBROW

She had to be 6 feet tall. She was huge and she was mean, and she wore big, brown polyester dress suits with brown plastic buttons. Her name was Mrs. Robinson. She was Cherryland Elementary School's new principal, and no one liked her. *Especially me.*

Besides several billion new playground rules, she imposed the toughest rule of all: ABSOLUTELY NO TALKING IN THE CAFETERIA.

She would stand stiffly in front of the stage where our winter concerts were held, megaphone in hand, picking off kids in the hot-lunch line. "NO TALKING IN THE CAFETERIA!" If we were lucky enough to make it through the inquisition, we would then take our lunch trays to a table and secretly communicate about the upcoming kickball game through eye and hand gestures.

But no, that wasn't enough! She had monitors on staff who had laminated pieces of colored construction paper. GREEN FOR THE QUIETS, RED FOR THE TALKERS. If a table got slapped with a red sign, recess was history. If Mrs. Robinson was in a *good mood*, the talkers would be allowed to move to the detention benches outside.

I was in the fifth grade, having attended Cherryland on and off since kindergarten. We moved a lot but always seemed to return to the s a m e neighborhood. I'd seen the passing of two principals, been through the hornet's-nest scare of '78, and o v e r s a w many a cupcake sale.

School had become my refuge.

It was always there when I came back.

MRS. ROBINSON'S RULE had already been in effect for over a week on the day I shaved off HALF of my *left eyebrow*. Cindy, before she dropped out of high school, would shave off BOTH of her eyebrows, then draw them back on with a makeup pencil.

Cindy was always called the pretty one.
She and Mom would spend private time together,
talking all night about private things, and I just assumed
it was about HAIR AND MAKEUP because there was
a **mirror** on the table between them. I wanted in.
SO I figured I'd start slow, to see if I liked it.

I stood in the hot-lunch line, free ticket in hand. My stomach was growling,
and my brain was dizzy from the many whispered questions about my half eyebrow.
"What happened?" "Why'd you do that?" "Will it grow back?"
Then I heard her. "YOUNG LADY," her voice echoed over the whispers.
"YOUNG LADY—YES, YOU THERE—COME TO THE FRONT OF THE LUNCHROOM. NOW!"

I looked up to see MRS. ROBINSON pointing right at me.
I walked forward, slightly confused. Without looking, she squeezed
her hand around my arm, holding me in place as she unceasingly struck her
commandments across an innocent field of open lunch boxes.

I don't quite remember what she said to me before she placed
me in a line with the other unfortunate talkers, but I do
remember the humiliation of being displayed in front
of the third through sixth grades with an eyebrow and a half.

I moved in a dream from the firing squad back over to
MRS. ROBINSON and her semiautomatic megaphone. Standing as
tall as I could, I spoke, telling her what a MEAN AND SCARY person
she was, and that her cafeteria rule was a bad one. It was my school,
NOT HERS. I was safe there, and
she was trying to change that.

I had started my period
on the morning of picture day, earlier that week.
Still a baby, I stood 5'6", with HIPS, BREASTS, AND BARBIE DOLLS.
I wore the same size shoe as my Mom. (*Sometimes I'd sneak out to school wearing her 5-inch-heel go-go boots.*) I was one of maybe 3 girls in my elementary school who had reached womanhood early.
I'd soon learn that "AUNT FLO" *was a lot more reliable than my mother.*

I spent the rest of that fateful day in the principal's office.
My Mom was found and called in. An "emergency conference" was held between MRS. ROBINSON, my mother, and the school counselor. Oh, and me too. It was decided that I was not responsible for my "*outburst,*" because I had just started my period and most definitely had PMS. At the end of our talk, everyone pretended to like each other again. MRS. ROBINSON gave me a *big hug* and reminded me to wipe from the front to the back after I "made potty."

That night, my Mom was around to go over the dos and don'ts of menstruation. She borrowed a couple of tampons from Cindy, but I was too MORTIFIED when she instructed me on how to use them.
Thankfully, the school had sent me home with a teen magazine and a box of sanitary napkins a few days before.

"*I got my period during one of the summers* I was sent to visit
your Grandma Mary in New York," my Mom recalled.
"She just handed me a pad and a belt and left it at that. I had a
tough time figuring it all out. We sure didn't have adhesive pads like this!
We had to attach ours to an elastic belt a bit bigger than a G-string!"

She dug through her makeup case while recalling bloody horror stories,
which I assumed I should note and never repeat. NO MORE borrowing my
girlfriends' clothes. *No more running around like a tomboy with the boys.*
No more swimming. She pulled a brown pencil from her makeup case
and cradled my chin in her hand, holding my face still.
I watched our reflection in the bathroom mirror as
she filled in my half brow.

"When I was a little older than you, I went with your Grandma Mary to
a tennis and swimming party at the estate of some of her and Grandpa Kinney's
important friends. When I changed into my swimming suit, I took off my pad and
belt and left them behind with my tennis clothes. Well, not an hour passed before
a pack of boys, headed by Nelson Rockefeller's son, came running out from the
dressing rooms over to where the girls and ladies were lounging, waving my bloody
pad in the air! 'Charlotte's got her period! Charlotte's got her period!'"

She stopped for a moment to examine her work.
She took a drag off her cigarette.

"My mother beat me
black and blue. I spent that
week using ice packs for my
cramps and my ass both!"

Hi Baby,

Mother called after you called us and a lot has been explained in my mind.
Now I understand why you are mad at her, I am too now. She did mess you kid's
up in some ways but Larry should of never signed the bond knowing that you got in
your mess by doing just that. Of course he loves you but it doesn't emprove
things by doing more wrong. Kinney and I knew things weren't right but we couldn't
see why.

Larry and Mother had planned to spend our 500 and only 100 on getting you
out. That too is wrobg Charlotte because Kinney works hard ofr his money. He is
a wonderfull person to raise my children and help thim in need. He had browed
that money, do you realize it takes us one year to save that much. And we lose
money every time we have to move. Do you also realize it has cost us 160 for
your checks and over 100 for phone calls and 80 we sent you (witch I heard you
tryed to buy a dryer with, the only reason we sent so much was to put on your
bills and get you out of a jam.) And if the money we browed wasn't returned I
Would have to live on 300 a month bills and all, why our rent alone is 125.

You two must learn every one works to get what they have, they deserve to
spend there own money. You two can't expect every one to hand money out ot you.
And if you don't like some one it isn't reason enough to cause them bills. Baby
learn to pay your own way and always remember reveenge is not fo us. We must
learn to forgive. And above all els I thought you would never lie to me again
and here you were lieing even then. The welfare didn't pay for that call. And
every time you have called at someone els home we get stuck with it. I will not
pay for any more, so when they called this time I said no. Mother said no too.
They called her while we were talking.

I will just have to stop you from calling if we recieve one more call from
the phone company. You can't afford it and neither can Mother or Kinney. It is
good to hear your voice and when you are troubled we would like to help our baby
but Kinney has never recieved one phone bill with out long distant calls on it,
not sence we hve been here. So no more please baby, we will just have to learn
to write.

I do want you to know we have put a few pieces together now. I owe Larry
and you an appolegy for what I have thought and for lessoning to mother to much
she is known for being a learand you don't do so bad eather, plus the fact Kinney
and I are so far away. So how can we know the truth when we hear,it.Baby try to
stop lieing and if you can't see a doctor. You can go to far with it you know.
You collect on what you put out and as long as you put out bad seeds you get mostly
weeds. O how can I help my baby, I love her so very much and I know she is going
all wrong and I can't seem to make her understand. Honey if we payed all bills
and kept getting her out of one jam to enother she would never learn her way.
Yet the whole thing is so hard she might wish to turn away from me for ever. Honey
we are by your side but you must learn even if it seems mean and cold. Remember
" Do unto others as you would have them do umto you."? Is it right to put calls on
others? Is that what you want done to you? Do you want to put out all your money
on someone els when you know it will be wasted and lost? As long as I have
been around you were getting things I never dreamed I could have..
    I know mother expected a lot from our money and she forgot your daddy is
way smarter than her or Larry. She promised she would put in the pot to get
Kinneys money, I guess your daddy fixed her red wagon. That money belongs to
your father and no one eles unless he says so.
    Mother said she wished Kinney was there and walk down the streets in his
uniform. She said that would get a few. "But" one, daddy would be to ashamed
to wear his uniform near her and the mess that was made. Two, if he was there
it wouldn't of been her side he would of been on, her head might of got in the
chopping block too. And I know alittle girl with the curl who would of been
sore on the bottom too. But her hurt wouldn't of been so sore as a few others
would of been ! I sould of had one too, because I forgot yo learned thattrash
from her ho se, but I wanted someone who I could let us know what was going on
and to help my baby if she had learned. Now all she has learned is to fight back
with more trash. No baby that isn't the way. Let me try to explain by useing one

oh how can i help my bab[...]
[...]love her so very much and i know she is gol[...]
[...]er h[...]
[...]rsta[...]
COMPANY

of my problems here. God sayes revenge is mine, here is how it works.

　　　You remember how many friends I have in bowling? Well one girl got jealous
so she got a bunch of new girls to lesson and theybelived her. I in return did
what was right. I even went out of my way to help the girls even more. They slammed
me, my children nd my homw. But mommie worked all the harder to help them. telling
all I loved all the girls i bowl with and it hurts me to see someone is mad at me.
Well the very girl who started it all told one of the girls I was the best secutary
the alley has. And slowly but surely every one of the girls were comeing back
to me and it made more friends. I have learned this way is better. O I had hives,
cryed even in my sleep. nd I am not over it by almile, in fact I had a back set
because I bowled 5 stricks in a row and took high game from her, our team took
her second place for teams, and worse yet I might take the alleys trophy for the
march of dimes sweepstakes and if that isn't enough we bowled her team that day
and took all four plus my bowler took her high series, and all from her. She hsd
them sewed up and my team striped her. It is just bowling, we bowled up a storm
and you can't get the pins unless you knock them down. Yet it is one type of revenge
even though we weren't trying but look what it has done. She always wanted to
het my spot, Well thats what she wanted, and baby it is all so untrue. Yes I
would like a trophy but who wouldn't, but hurt her no ! So you see doing things
for others, even if it hurts, always pays off. Can you see what I am trying to
explain? Yo learned at mothers the wrong way and yo have got deeper and deeper
now try my way baby. It is the harder way but what big crops you get in return.
What ever you put out that is what is returned. So baby plant good seeds and good
tho ghts. I am not perfect in fact I too have to learn my lessons over again. And
I am so far off yet it is hard to do right, I wrong others often and I am far
from being a good christia ,But I have learned this much and I would like my children
to learn it too because it is good. Try to understand baby and reread this letter
because it is long and I want you to remember every bit. I do love my baby !

　　　　　　　　　　　　　　　　　　　　　　　Minnie

GRAVIDITY

I was 11 and flexible.
I was able to fit between the
side wall of our rental and
the apartment wall next door.
I'd rest my back on one and
climb my legs up the other,
UNTIL I MADE A HUMAN L, and then I would stay there, suspended.

*When I looked up, I could see my Dad's brown eyes
peeking out from behind a microscope slide of stars.*

There is something about those places where we go to cry.

BOBBY LEFT FOR GOOD FIRST, *not yet 18*, to join the armed forces with my Mom's approval
and, unbeknownst to him, her social security number. My Mom waved goodbye
with her casted forearm, the arm she'd broken just a few weeks earlier over
my brother's head. He signed his name with a big black indelible-ink marker
and drew a heart, which got SMALLER AND SMALLER as the basic-training
truck drove away *toward a LIFE spent in institutions.*

My Mom shrugged with pride.
"HE WAS SO HIGH, HE DIDN'T FEEL A THING."

CINDY LEFT SECOND, *wearing her snug bridal dress*,
in the arms of an AWOL Marine. I thought that would be
the last time I'd see her, draped in lace, billowing and full of LIFE.
I hoped for a second that she might float away and break free from us.

Up, up . . . above the smells of the tomato cannery and the tortilla factory.
Out, out . . . beyond the TRACKS and the BAY, and above the GOLDEN GATE.
Cindy, ascending—
in her thrift-store wedding gown,
through the pregnant fog. . . .

But beyond those fluffy clouds of possibility—
between the blue of hope and light—
CUT A LINE OF YELLOW CRANK.
It kept her eternally connected to our mother.

Cindy gave birth one month after her sixteenth
birthday. Mom whispered to me that
Cindy had had twins. *"One died."* Mom said
that she and the doctors decided to keep this news
from Cindy because of her fragile condition.

What condition that was, only Mom knew.

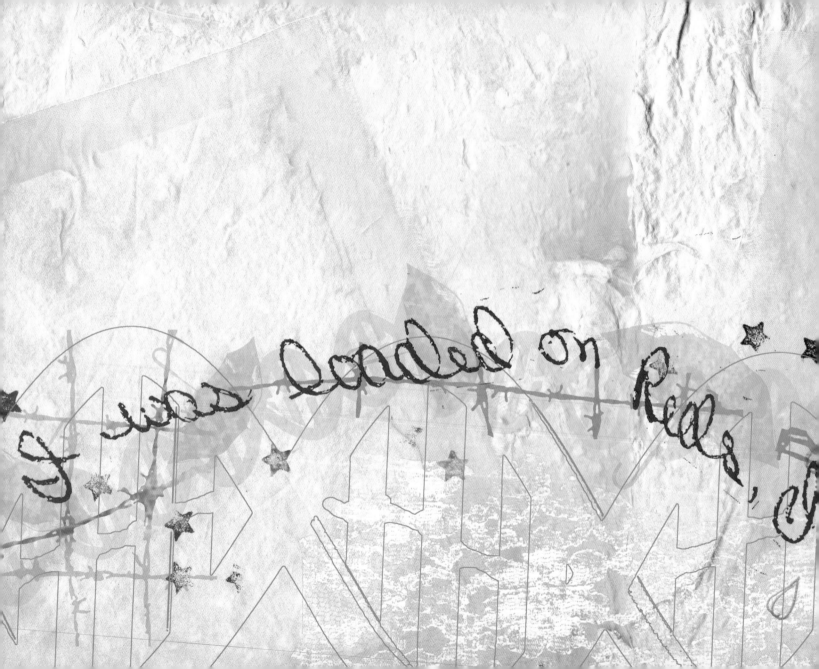

I was loaded on Reds,

I think.

think.

DETACHED

David Hans Schnabel repeated the
same words he'd said in that letter.
Funny, I knew it was him when the
phone rang. I caught a deep breath
before I picked it up, and I detached.

"Hey, Lil' Sister."

I forgot he used to call me that.

David Hans Schnabel said he had been hauling apples since
Holly Sugar shut down. That was the sugar plant where my
Dad worked. I didn't know David had worked there, too.

Mom would drive me up and over Patterson Pass;

I could see the huge concrete silos jutting up from

the farmland. Their shadows stretched out on one side.

"That's where your Daddy worked," she'd say.

David Hans Schnabel said he hauled the apples in
a big rig, as far as the Shirley Temple Black Estate,
sometimes farther. *"Watsonville,"* he said.

Yes, two sugar silos, towering over the Tracy valley.

Bright white on the side that reflected the sun, making

my eyes well up. *"Almost there,"* Mom would say.

David Hans Schnabel said his hours on the road are long. He sleeps in his mother's basement. She is 96. He looks after her. He said years ago he drove past my great-grandma's house, where Cindy lives now, but never stopped.

I felt like those silos were mine. They were my Dad's
and they were mine. I can't imagine their being gone.
How will giants find their graveyard?

*"Did you know back then? About me possibly
being your kid?"* **I asked.** "Yeah, Cori, I knew."

HE SAID . . .

**"Your mother and I had been
going out long before David Crooks
was around. We still saw each other
when she started up with him. . . ."**

"David Crooks accused a lot of guys
of sleeping with your mother, but he
never said a word of it to me. He didn't
have a problem with me. . . ."

"When I found out David Crooks had wrecked his VW and died, I asked your mother
to marry me, 'cept she didn't want me. She said to leave things as they were. She said
she was gonna get death benefits for you, and she didn't want me to say anything about
us. . . . She didn't want me to screw it up."

He said my Dad was a drunk.
HE SAID A LOT OF THINGS.

gregory 3/58

BABY #1

When he was 10,
he came back to the house where my mother was raised.

Where the heat of the past was shaded by her dense tangerine trees—
where her fruit hung as low as a child could jump.

He said Mom called him out from nowhere.
"I guess we should get to know each other."

She never explained why she left him behind, blanketed, bundled, blue—but breathing.
She didn't leave him on the rich doorstep of a childless couple. She did not gently lay
him in a basket she wove, setting him adrift along a river of reeds.
She left him in a barn—quite possibly the barn where he was conceived.
Where neighborhood boys and neighborhood girls met
and kept neighborly secrets.

She was 16.
She didn't want to be married.
SHE LIKED TO RIDE MOTORCYCLES.

"For a long time, I thought she left because of my seizures," he said.

And, like my big brother said, after 3 months of promises, she left again.
It would be a lifetime before he ever returned to that house.

ALCATRAZ

When my Mom found out my class would be going on a tour of ALCATRAZ for our eighth-grade field trip, she volunteered.

During our tour, she corrected the docent several times.

He was telling it all wrong.

Eventually she explained that she

had once spent the night at the

maximum-security prison.

You see, her stepfather, whom Grandma Mary called "Kinney," was a naval officer who had an old friendship with the warden.

The warden's wife had invited the whole family to a dinner party, which, of course, would be at their residence on the island, long before any Indians burned it down.

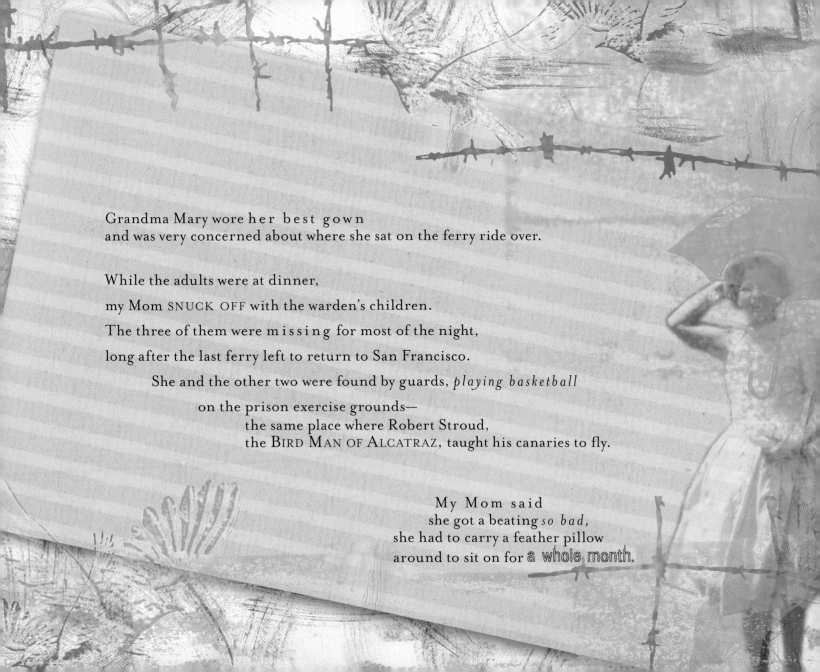

Grandma Mary wore her best gown
and was very concerned about where she sat on the ferry ride over.

While the adults were at dinner,

my Mom SNUCK OFF with the warden's children.

The three of them were missing for most of the night,

long after the last ferry left to return to San Francisco.

She and the other two were found by guards, *playing basketball*

on the prison exercise grounds—
the same place where Robert Stroud,
the BIRD MAN OF ALCATRAZ, taught his canaries to fly.

My Mom said
she got a beating *so bad*,
she had to carry a feather pillow
around to sit on for a whole month.

SOME OF WHAT HE LEFT ME

It sat on my Mom's knickknack shelf for years. My Daddy gave it to her just before he died. She finally passed it down to me when I was a teen, when I promised I would never burn incense in it. *I still have it. It sits on a special shelf in my house, next to a picture of him.*

a Hindu god

Sulfasuxidine.
I tablet every 3 hours.
Keep out of reach of
children. 6/9/70 . . .
13 days before
the accident.

a bottle of pills

For years, I remembered
this lighter as a ZIPPO, but
it's a CHAMP. The flint still
shoots off sparks. I think
of his hands. He held this
in his hands.

a lighter

a bent spoon

My Dad could bend spoons. I heard a few spoon stories. One was about how he'd crack ice cubes for me to teethe on. The story goes, he'd hold a few solid cubes in his hand and hit them with the back of a spoon . . . and they'd crack into perfect teething-size pieces. Anytime I need to break ice, I think of him and how strong his hands must have been. As for this spoon—my Daddy bent it for me so I could eat dinner like a "big girl"

. . . but i don't have his hard hat.

No Hard Hat

Long before sugar was refined,
men boiled stalks of sugarcane down
until they were chicken bones,
until a sweet syrup, the envy of bees,
grew and then reduced—
bubbled and then *relaxed*.

And those reductions,
reductions of thick, glossy nectar,

were carefully divided and dispersed
into deep waiting pots,
hot poured into cool—
making a sweet steam that would stick to the skin
and leave a taste.

And while those men were at rest,
and while those pots cooled,
crystals grew and formed and then were scraped out of the bellies
by small hands,
small cupped hands,
with tiny reaching fingers.
Tiny sneaking fingers
whose only task—after easing the burns—
was to sprinkle the sugar over halved peaches
for their beloved mothers.

When he came home

from the sugar plant

he'd open the door a crack,

he'd put his hard hat in,

he'd close the door and wait.

If she opened the door

and threw the hat back,

she was still boiling.

She was still raging.

She was still steaming.

So he and his hat

would take a cold step

AND HEAD FOR THE BAR.

People have said
my Daddy loved
hardheaded women.

Maybe Mom boiled down,
like sweet sugar juice.

SHOE LOTTERY

"Hi, Cori? This is Carla, David Schnabel's daughter. My Dad told me to call and get your birth date so he can play it along with Kimmy's and mine in the lotto."

That's exactly what she said when she called me back a couple of days after we first spoke.

"So . . . you know who I am?"

Who I might be.

"Yeah, I figured it out. . . . Hi."

We spoke for over an hour. She shared her life, defining herself by
the men she loved, those men who d i d n ' t s t a y, how loving always left
her a l o n e. *Two babies.* Two fathers. BOTH IN PRISON.

D r u g s. Mistakes. *Christianity.*

"I hope my Dad doesn't love you more than me," she s a i d.

It never seems to be any different.
We can know onlywhat we know.
We can't walk that mile if the shoes are too small.

"Your Dad said he'd do a DNA test with me—

as soon as the apple harvest slows down a little.

So he's going to call when he's ready. . . . "

Your Daddy, Baby. Your Daddy.

MY DARLING CLEMENTINE

Maybe it was Cindy's being gone that caused Mom to start taking chances.

Maybe it was my not needing her that caused her to become so careless.

Over the next few months, Mom offered all

that she had, including herself,

to our landlord . . .

and one day I came home

to an EMPTY HOUSE.

I think that was the time I found out.
Right before my twelfth birthday.
We were driving down Meekland Ave. when she said it.
Two men—one of two men.
David Hans Schnabel wasn't my Dad's best friend after all.

AS WE TURNED ONTO SUNSET AVE.,
a crack opened in me and her words fell straight down into it.
"I was waiting for the right time," she said,
clicking her turn signal. *Clacking her teeth.*

We stood there together, at the edge of my crack.
She held my hand—to save herself. She thought I'd push her in.
I THOUGHT IT'D BE BETTER TO LEAVE HER OUT.

I covered that crack quickly. I had rehearsed.
I sealed it up and saved it. My back never broke.

After circling the block, she pulled up to

Cindy's apartment. I took the grocery bags

filled with my clothes and walked to her door.

Once I was inside, I found a place to sit.

I've always been on a Summer.

SLEEPWALKING

She did a line

and I watched her sew thread into panels of brown fabric that formed curtains that draped and clothing that covered. EACH STITCH CORRECT.

She did a line
and I watched her build shelves from one-by-eights and cement blocks, so careful to let the wood stain dry completely.

No book forgotten. Organized by subject, alphabetized, then sorted by height and by color.

She did a line

and I watched her build model ships, spend sleepless nights
gluing miniature masts onto Spanish galleons:
the *Pinta*, the *Niña*, the *Santa Maria*.

She did a line

and I watched her pour plaster into exact molds
of conquistadors,
Aztec calendars,
and naughty bathroom plaques
that decorated our walls
and charmed those men.

*"If you sprinkle,
When you tinkle,
Be a sweetie,
Wipe the seatie."*

She did a line

AND I WATCHED HER PRECISELY PAD AND COVER
photo albums filled full of her 7 children—
children that she abandoned in barns,
children that she bore in prisons,
children that she never claimed—
babies that *reached up*
and out FROM CRIB PAGES AS . . . .

She did a line

and I watched her paint, GOLD-LEAF, and
antique her past in brilliant, worthy colors,
gilding new lies and aging them to fit the present.

And when all those lines she did were done,

I watched from very far away
when she was finally able

to sleep.

BABY AND THE BATHWATER

David Hans Schnabel
said he'd take the DNA test
as soon as the season slowed,
as soon as he wasn't driving
those 13 hour shifts—

AS SOON AS HE STOPPED DREAMING
OF HAULING APPLES,
and of my mother's face.

"Is it a blood test?"

"No, it's a cotton-swab test;
       you just swipe the inside of your cheek
       with a Q-tip-type thingy and mail it
       to the lab. You don't have to go anywhere
       official. I could order the test and have it
       here within 3 days—
              then we could get together, do
              the test, and next-day-air it.
              I could have the ANSWER by the
              end of the week."

"You know, Cori, I could go ahead and pay for half of the test," he said.

"No, no . . . I've got it covered."

**"You know, I don't want you to think I'm trying to get out of it
or anything like that."**

      "No, it's okay. I completely understand—you gotta
         take the work when you can get it.
         You just let me know when you're ready,
         and I'll order the test."

I don't know why I lied.

I had the test already.

It was good for 3 years.

THURSDAY / Aug. 23

A foster family got a call from Child
Services about twin girls born to a
mother in prison. That foster mom
loved those little girls, and when she
heard of an older brother out there
in the cold system, she found him
and brought the 3 together.
And there they stayed—with a
mom and dad who wanted them.

peter 5/59

BABY #2

SOMETIMES NO ONE KNOWS
EXCEPT THAT OLD HOUSE.

She holds all of her pictures
down the stairs,
in the corners of her pockets—
where they are safe and secret.

A life can start and end before the right person grabs a pen
and puts a name to a face, writes a date and a place on the back.

You were here.

What happened? I don't know what happened to you . . . as a baby.
I don't know if you lived with Mom until she went to prison.
I don't know how long you were in the system—if t e m p o r a r y families
have photos of you with t e m p o r a r y brothers and sisters.

I don't know who my brother is in the pictures.
So I can't be the one to label them.

Our MOTHER told me that you had been adopted . . .
but someone said that it wasn't exactly true.
She wouldn't let go of you when they asked—
but she wouldn't take you, either—
just like those unsigned pictures
in the careworn pockets of t h a t o l d h o u s e.

2 YEARS, A COUCH, AND A BIRTHDAY

1. Cindy's Couch.

It had to be 8 feet long. It was a boxy, '70s "feelings" sort of couch. She had gotten it at the Purple Heart Thrift Store. The fabric was a TEXTURED PLAID, with browns and straw-colored polyester yarns. It was pretty *scratchy*.

The couch was so long that someone could smoke a bowl on the other end and not wake me up.
     In the mornings I would pull the couch out to plug in my blow dryer.

2. Great-Grandmother's Couch:

She called it a CHESTERFIELD.
The velvety fabric was protected by p o u n d s of
crocheted blankets that you could wiggle your toes
through. On top of those crocheted blankets sat
Grandma's doll collection.
12 plastic, life-size dolls, sitting happily.

Their eyes would close when you laid them down.
I was sure to do that every night—I'd straighten their legs
and lay them down on the floor. I'd sleep with my face to the back cushion
so I couldn't see them.
In the morning I'd set them back on the
CHESTERFIELD, nice and pretty,
before I left for school.

3. Aunt Kelly's Couch:

She had a rust-colored, sectional, L-shaped couch. It had a low back, with fat, round, matching cushions. Each square section had a big wake-you-up-in-the-middle-of-the-night-if-you-lay-on-it button lodged in the center. She'd leave a stack of sheets for me to cover everything with. She liked her apartment fancy. She had one of those wax-dripping, Venus de Milo statuette lamps hanging in the corner, and a nude painting of herself on all fours, framed in gold, hanging above her big brass bed. There was no evidence of my cousin, who was in and out of foster care and Youth Authority most of his life. In the morning, I'd straighten up, do Aunt Kelly's dishes, pack all of my belongings, and take them with me. She was nice when I was just visiting. She showed me how to sculpt my eyebrows. She said to never pluck on the top.
Yeah, she was real nice when she wasn't drinking.

4. Ronnie's Couch:

I'd stay with my mother there sometimes. She had two couches. Mom would sleep on one, and I would sleep on the other.

5. Missy's Couch:

Missy was my best friend. We met playing tetherball in fourth grade. Her couch had a high back and wooden armrests. One of those country couches.

HER MOM, BETSY, was a Topanga Canyon hippie turned born-again.

She went to church FOUR TIMES a week and served me my first bowl of brown rice. I was always welcome there, and never had to sleep on the couch. I also never needed to set my alarm clock, because Betsy woke the house up at sunrise, *singing to Jesus.*

6. Some Man's Couch:

I TURNED 14 ON HIS COUCH. It was a *shiny*, high-backed, black leather sofa. I think it was new.

He didn't like the idea of my being there that night, but I was sick. My Mom said she was staying with him in exchange for cleaning his house, except she slept in his room.
She checked in on me a few times that night,
and took me back to CINDY'S COUCH early the next morning.

OWLS IN SAND

POST CARD

MADE IN U.S.A.

CORRESPONDENCE · ADDRESS

PLACE STAMP HERE

AGFA ANSCO ★ ★ ★

The sands of Don Castro
were poured along the shore
like ice into water.

The two so transparent against each other,

as if the grains had been molded

in a metal tray

that some thirsty construction worker

grabbed from MOTHER NATURE'S

olive green Frigidaire—

when he cracked the frosty lever,

the pieces fell, and he created a beach

in the middle of

SPANISH SUBURBIA.

That's where I, as
a child, first met

David Hans Schnabel.

As summer gave way to October
and the melting corners cooled,
he was the "tall drink of water"
at that man-made lake.

He let me cover him
up to his head in sand.
HE BOUGHT ME A TACO AND A LIME JARRITOS.
He looked at me twice when I spoke.
THAT MADE ME LOVE HIM.

"Cori," I hear her say, again and again,
"this is David.
He was your Daddy's friend."

rinse subject's mouth three tim

le from one individual at a time.

6.   Open one of the sample tubes with a Tamper
THE FOAM TIP. Collect tissue by
Catch-All™ sample collection swab fi
inside of each cheek 30 tim
certain to move the b
cheek surfaces. (Figure)

of the sample tubes. DO NO
M TIP. Collect tissue by r the
M sample collection swab firmly the
ch cheek 30 times about 1 minute. Be
over the

collection tube with the num
on the adjacent Tamper Seals
individual to be tested. (E

**September is almost over,
and I've not heard from him again.**

Now the wait buries me.

I am picking grains of sand from my shoes.
I am uncovering the past and looking too
closely at those sandy pictures.

I HAVE THE WORLD'S MOST PERFECT FATHER, *the
breath in my moments of suffocation,*
who is a dead ghost.

AND I HAVE THE WORLD'S WORST FATHER,
whom I've seen 4 times, who has been no more than
a name I spell wrong, *but who is alive.*

I turn the hourglass over and over.
I read and reread the directions to the DNA test.

I weigh that heavy weight.

Repeat steps 5 and 7 for the **same individual** **using a fresh swab.**

Allow the swabs to dry at room temperature for 2 hours, or until completely dry, before step 10.

Insert Catch-All™ sample collection swabs in the appropriately labeled tubes and reassemble.

Attach the corresponding Tamper Seal **firmly** ~~ver the area where the tube portions meet,~~ ~~sure~~ the Tamper Seal Number is visible ~~igure 5).~~

~~nd~~ Consent Form, (Figure 6).

Legal Tests: Complete the <u>SWBIC - Chain of</u> <u>Custody and Analysis Request</u> and <u>Informed</u> <u>Consent and Sample Control Form,</u> (examples included if you requested legal test kit).

Figure 6

14. Retain the pink copy of the <u>SWBIC -</u> <u>Documentation and Consent Form</u> fo~~r~~ records.

15. Package the samples with the white and ~~co~~pies of the <u>SWBIC - Sample Documentati</u> <u>Consent Form</u> in the padded envelope an~~d~~ immediately, (Figure 7).

Figure 7

"save these labels Co

THE FINEST A~~~~

~~nts\Forms\F-015 REV~~

DRIVING LESSONS

Mom said that she knew her father.

He was a bread baker. He lived
and worked in San Francisco,
where he chased her 6 older
half-brothers along the rise and fall
of sourdough hills, way back when.

Leonardo Angelo was his name.
He seduced my 18-year-old GRANDMA MARY
with his accent and European charm.
Then he broke her heart
by professing undying love
for his wife of 25 YEARS.

Mom said he was from Sicily.
Stocky, strong, and dark—SO DON'T EVER THINK
OF MESSING WITH HIS LITTLE GIRL.

Later, when people questioned her,
she said he was from n o r t h e r n I t a l y.
Lean, swift, and cool. That's why Mom had blue eyes.

"There are a lot of blondes in Venice," s h e ' d s a y,
AND DON'T THINK HE DIDN'T HAVE CONNECTIONS.

Her father named her CEANNE, after *Saint Ceanne*, a nun
who witnessed the image of the ARCHANGEL GABRIEL while
staring up into the face of *Michelangelo's* DAVID.

They say Saint Ceanne was an ecstatic, so overwhelmed with

mankind's reverence for the divine that she fainted at David's

marble feet. Thirteen days later, she awoke from her malady.

When the doctors examined her, they found that her back was

covered in a red yeast. It was said that the rash

soon sprouted white feathers. It was also said

that she grew full wings that carried her

up above her deathbed and flew her toward

the blue heaven, to touch the hand of God.

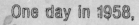

One day in 1958,

Leonardo Angelo grew tired of driving across the bay to fetch his daughter for weekend visits, AND SO HAD HIS WIFE.

One Sunday after Mass, at which the deacon expounded upon the virtues of fidelity, L e o n a r d o finally gave in and announced that CeAnne should learn to drive. **"All American girls drive."**

This pleased the wife.

Three of her half dozen half-brothers,

M a r i o ,   D o n a t e l l o ,   a n d   L u i g i ,

drove her to North Beach and left her

at the top of Lombard Street with their

daddy's white Edsel. As they walked away,

Mario turned and threw her the keys,

"Geta yourselfa home."

Somehow, through a thick paste of clouds,
CeAnne glided down safely.

Through a series of lefts and rights, she descended
"THE CROOKEDEST STREET IN THE WORLD."
Some say an unseen hand, *possibly the feathered
hand of her namesake,* reached down and shifted—
just as she stepped on the clutch.

"Then why does Great-Grandma call you Charlotte?" I asked.

"CeAnne is the Italian name for Charlotte."

That's what she said, way back when.

Another time she said her father
was listed in the phone book under the
surname LUSTER. She said he lived
in the *rundown trailer park* up the road
from the house where she was raised.

She said she hoped he'd died
of emphysema.

THE ABORTION

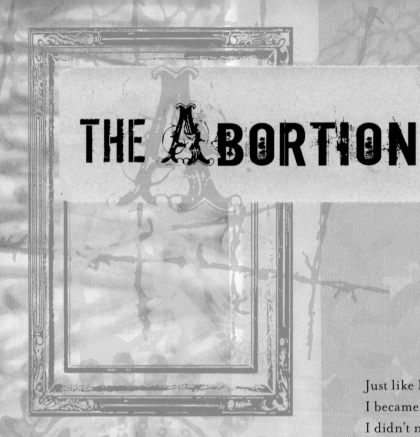

*She was 16 years and 10 months old
when she had Greg.*

She was 18 years old when she gave birth to Pete.

*She was 18 and 11 months
when she bore the twins in prison.*

She was 21 years and 6 months when she had Bob,
23 and 8 with Cindy, and 28 years old
and some when she had me.

All before 1973.

Just like Mom,
I became pregnant at a time when
I didn't necessarily want to be.
It was strange, too,
because I knew immediately—
right when it happened.
I felt it, a deep, deep
wrong in my body.
I didn't need to take a home test.
I made an appointment with an ob-gyn
and terminated the pregnancy. I never thought twice about it,
nor did I ever regret my decision.

Cori

All those things for a mother
to serve a daughter are great, arn't
they? I wish I could have been
that kind of mother.! But I'm
just me. Lots of dreams little
substance.

But theres what you do
have my dear. My Love
My Trust
and
My Deepest Respect

Mom

 WORD PROBLEMS

I AM FIVE YEARS YOUNGER THAN DENNIS CROOKS, AND ONE AND A HALF YEARS YOUNGER THAN RON.

I AM EIGHT MONTHS YOUNGER THAN KIMMY SCHNABEL, AND TWO YEARS OLDER THAN CARLA.

David Hans Schnabel IS ON AN APPLE TRAIN, TRAVELING AT A SPEED OF 100 KM/H. HE IS PASSED BY THE GHOST OF DAVID CROOKS, WHO IS ON A PEACH TRAIN TRAVELING IN THE SAME DIRECTION, AT A CONSTANT SPEED. TEN SECONDS AFTER DAVID CROOKS'S GHOST PASSES *David Hans Schnabel*, THEIR TRAINS ARE 100 M APART. WHAT IS THE SPEED OF DAVID CROOKS'S TRAIN IN KM/H?

Which one is my father?

I called Carla. I thought I might find a way to get that train rolling. Maybe she had some pull with her daddy.

We talked about what we look like.

I'm pretty tall, 5′10″, but she's short,

5′4″. I have blue eyes, but she has brown.

Deep set? Yes. High cheekbones? Yes.

Kimmy has a Drew Barrymore chin. . . .

Yes, I do too. But so did my Mom.

Does Kimmy know about me?
No. They hadn't spoken in 9 years,
      until last July. Carla said she
  g r a d u a t e d from some sort of
program and Kimmy flew out
    from Virginia to celebrate.

Hasn't talked to her since, though.
Carla doesn't want her mom to
find out about me, so she thinks
  IT'S BEST TO WAIT.

Yeah.
FEELS LIKE A LIE.

**I told her I'd send her
some pictures.**

She said that she hopes we are sisters.
She said that if the test is positive
and we are indeed blood,
then there's no letting go after that.

THAT FEELS WEIRD.

I think of Dennis and Ron,
my Dad's sons, b i g b r o t h e r s to this *little sister.*

Their mama was a traveler.

They never spent too long in school.
    Their wives still write me Christmas cards.
    I haven't exactly told them what's going on.

Yeah, I think it's best to wait.

 MOVIE HOUSE

ONCE, twice, *a couple different times,*
ENOUGH TO MAKE ME CHECK,
I'd walk out of sixth-period freshman English
and see my mother across the quad of my school,
leaning against the front of her car,
holding her cigarette—
that way that she held it.

"Hey, kidda."

We'd park in fast-food parking lots,
eat Chicken Supremes, and listen to the CB RADIO.

Sometimes I'd fall asleep.
She'd grab a blanket and pillow from the back seat.
"Breaker, breaker, Lady 8 Ball . . . what's your 10/40?"
Crackle, hum, hiss.
I knew that she went to meet these men
after she dropped me off.

But when she didn't,
she'd take me to the second-run theater.
We'd get 25-cent bags of popcorn with
extra butter and watch last year's film
from choice 1940s seats.

She'd flick on a penlight and do logic puzzles.
"The X's mean no and the dots mean yes."
Midmovie, she would whisper to me,
"I'm going to go have a cigarette."
She always came back at the end—EXCEPT FOR THE TIME WHEN SHE DIDN'T.

Looking up at the screen, I see the main character LOCKING
a garage door from the inside I hear the sound of
a car engine a car door opens she climbs
inside **she lies down she** *closes* her eyes to inhale MOM
RUSHES UP and out the penlight rolls down the aisle *its light hitting*
row after row after row she runs and
runs but doesn't forget her
CIGARETTE. . . .

The lights from her car rolling in woke me up that night.
I opened the door quietly—to her smoke and her tears.
"That is how my mother died."

She and I curled up real close on Great-Grandma's

Chesterfield. I cried tears for my grandmother as

I traced the scar on my mother's wrist and the dolls

slept quietly on the floor, eyes closed, in the house
where my Mom
was raised.

the twins 4/60

BABIES #3 & #4

Marsha tells her story of when she was a twin.

Of when she saw reflections

of herself in icy puddles

and thought they were her sister.

Her face is so much hers now.
But it's their story,
taking place during a wet Oregon winter,
      galoshes on the playground,
           umbrellas and hooded coats.
She started sentences *and Jan finished them*
and Jan finished them.

IT'S A STORY WHERE
matriarchs sing, and dowagers flutter from
the trees of an old woman's fingers—
swaying her warm, breezy come hithers
as the winter withers.
She's there behind the chainlink fence, Jan—
she wants us to come over.

When Marsha speaks now
I hear three voices.
Mine and hers.
They believed Great-Grandma
was coming to take them home,
but the bell rang,
the birds flew, winter ended—
and loss descended.

Marsha tells her story....

Foster girls

foster curls

they lost Father

they lost Mother—

and soon one

would lose the other.

THE SCIENCE FAIR LIE

The Science Fair Lie happened in the same location as my first lie, except not in the field.

It was in the classroom.

The year I took lab, I sat next to Tom. He was a long-haired rocker dude who drove a jacked-up, primered '79 Charger with two performance-size speakers taking up his back seats. (*A skinny girl might have been able to slide between them if she was wearing spandex.*) Most days, I'd hear him rounding the corner on B Street when I got off the bus.

Tom would pick me up and we'd go pick up donuts and eat them in his car, waiting for school to start. Tom liked to play his tape deck right as the bell for first period rang. He'd turn his stereo up to 10 so the first few dongs of the AC/DC song "Hells Bells" would echo through the quad.

I DID WELL IN HIGH SCHOOL, WHEN I WAS THERE.

I had too much life to juggle.

Watching my sister's kids,
tracking down my mother,
WORKING, and trying to come off
as a teenage girl to my friends.

I did school when I was there, because there
was no room to do school outside of school.

In between, I stole my moments.

I lied to you, Ms. Jenkins.

I fabricated my science fair project.

It was all fake.

I never borrowed my great-grandmother's
seeing-eye cane, and I never tapped my way into
7-11s across town, *thinking I was paying
for a soda with a $10 bill when I was
actually handing over a $20 bill.*

When you asked me to come up
in front of the class and share
my hypothesis with everyone,
         I FELT LITTLE GUILT.

I was really screwed up, Ms. Jenkins.

        I am so sorry.

Do you remember my hypothesis?
It was a special one, at least to me.

"THE ESSENTIAL NATURE OF PEOPLE IS HONEST."

Even then, I believed in the good,
Ms. Jenkins, even if I did make it up.

I was a funny girl who found a moment's
solace in an imaginary world filled with
honest 7-11 cashiers. All 8 of them alerted
the "blind me" to my error and gave me back
the correct change.

I guess I could give you excuses, like that I didn't have time
to do the project. Maybe I just didn't want to know the truth.
In the end, whatever the reason, *it was a lie.*

That's why I brought you a
glazed donut.

MY STRANGE NOSE

end of september

I spoke with Carla again.

She stared at my
pictures for a long time—
she said she wanted to find her face in them.

"I think you have my nose."

"So . . . we look alike?"

**"Yeah . . . well . . . no. You know,
I don't know."**

*She said she hadn't quite gotten around
to sending me pictures, but would soon.*

Da, Dada, Daddy,
Dad, PAPA, POPS, *Pappy*,
   Father, The guy who I thought was my
   Father, The man who could be my Father,
MY POSSIBLE DAD/S, Your Dad, *Some dude my*
   Mom fucked,
A sperm donor,
A biological
   father,
      Daddy-o....

**Remember how I said the guy
who I thought was my _____
might not actually be my_____?**

Carla said her dad took my picture, along
with one of her and her sister, down to
the truck lot where drivers collect their
itineraries and set out to fill up their big rigs.

She said he showed our pictures to the other men who
haul loads of Crispin, Braeburn, and Red Delicious apples
through the torn tires scattered along I-5.

"You got three beautiful daughters,"
she said he said they said.

APPLE SEASON IS OVER NOW,
AND LAYOFFS ARE IMMINENT.

Carla said her dad was talking
about picking up some T-bones
and coming out to my place to
grill them up.

He's sure to have work for the rest

of the month—but possibly the first

weekend of next month, we . . .

Carla said she'll make an apple pie.

**"So . . . um . . .
you can get that
test done, too."**

I don't expect you to be perfect

no one is perfect

HANOI JANE VS. My Mom

I was one of those kids who watched old movies.

I'd pick MGM over Hanna-Barbera any Saturday morning. I guess you could say I had a fondness for widescreen and three-strip processes.

One Saturday I was curled up on the couch, watching *BAREFOOT IN THE PARK*, when my Mom came in and commanded that I "Shut that crap off!"

I'D SEE THE STORY
IN MY MIND BEFORE SHE'D SAY IT
    (with surround sound and subtitles),
along with all her other stories about DOING TIME,
status fights, and toothbrush/pen-ink tattoos.
    (She had a heart with the name Don on her swaying hip.)

"Jane Fonda is a piece of shit!" she'd growl.

Then the story would unfold . . .

of how the actress had been arrested for "protesting the war" . . .

of how she was ushered through my mother's cell block . . .

of how Jane made the PEACE SIGN as she passed . . .

and how my Mom jumped her in the showers and *broke her fingers.*

"Yeah, I kicked her ass"
   . . . IN GLORIOUS TECHNICOLOR!

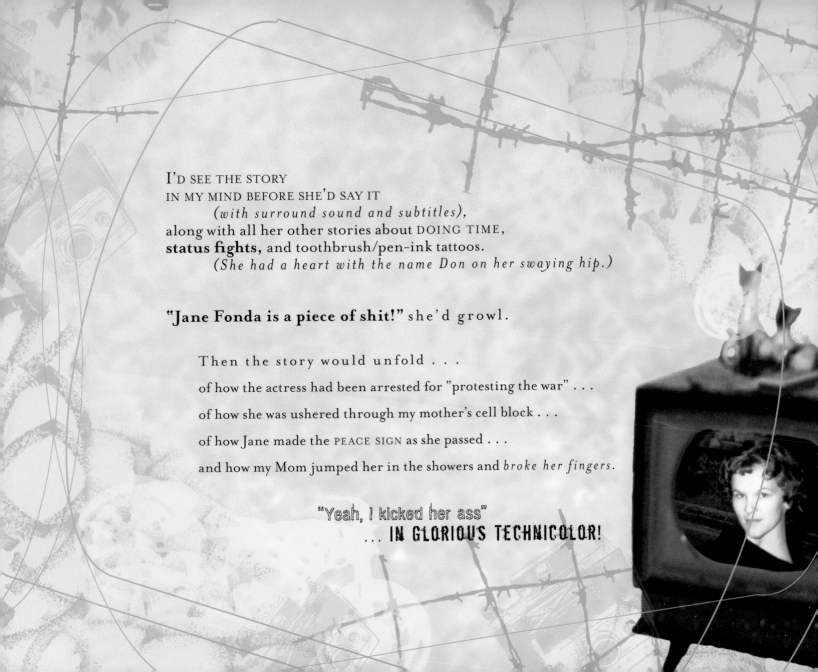

THE OTHER GRANDMOTHER

Those trips over Patterson Pass,
where we'd stop and get grave flowers
FROM THE PORTUGUESE MAN—
where my mother would breathe *smoke and regret*
and I would sit on my knees and talk to my father's ghost—

almost always ended with a visit to

my two paternal grandmothers.

They lived side by side in a manless house filled with the
memories of men. Two round crones anchored to the corner
by my GRANDPA PORTER'S boat, still dry-docked in the
backyard, where the grass was never watered and the
tools were where he'd left them.

120

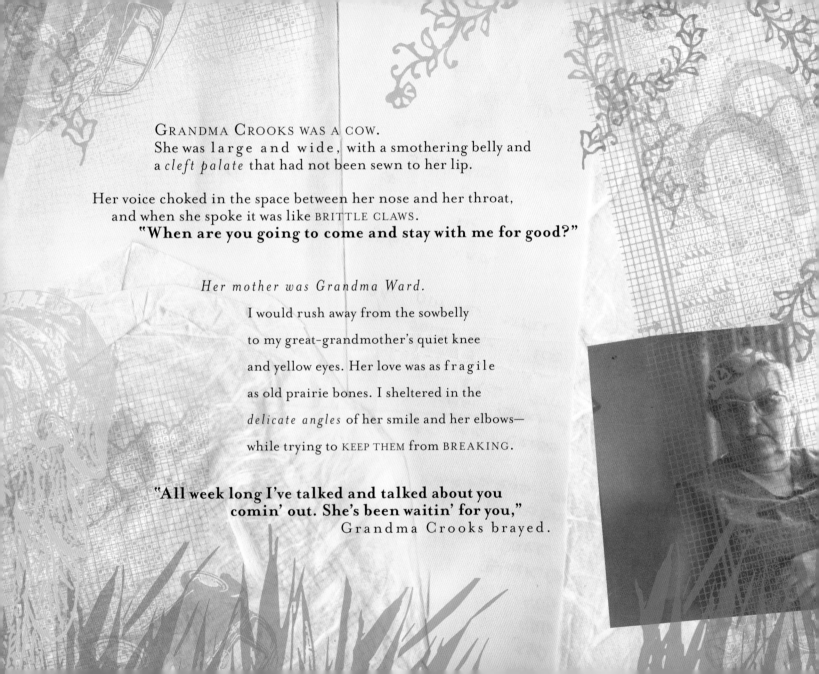

GRANDMA CROOKS WAS A COW.
She was large and wide, with a smothering belly and
a *cleft palate* that had not been sewn to her lip.

Her voice choked in the space between her nose and her throat,
and when she spoke it was like BRITTLE CLAWS.
"When are you going to come and stay with me for good?"

Her mother was Grandma Ward.

I would rush away from the sowbelly

to my great-grandmother's quiet knee

and yellow eyes. Her love was as *fragile*

as old prairie bones. I sheltered in the

delicate angles of her smile and her elbows—

while trying to KEEP THEM from BREAKING.

**"All week long I've talked and talked about you
comin' out. She's been waitin' for you,"**
Grandma Crooks brayed.

The silence of
Grandma Ward
was clear to me. I would cuddle onto her lap,

run my fingers along her silver braids,

and look into her Indian face.

She had brown spotted patches along her cheeks, *like a wild pony.*

After Grandma Ward passed away,
visits to Patterson were close to
UNBEARABLE.

I'd stick my nose in coloring books

and not look up when Grandma Crooks

spoke—so as not to see her voice strike

like crushed trumpets out of that space

between the opening in her lip.

The last time I saw/heard her was at Christmastime.
I believe I was in fourth grade . . . '79?

Mom had shown me how to make a plaster Christmas tree
statuette from a rubber mold. I poured it and painted
it pearly green with red and gold bulbs. I gave it to my
Grandma Crooks, who had recently found comfort at
the local Kingdom Hall.

"I'll keep it, but I won't worship it," she mooed.

Mom came back in from
having a smoke with grocery
bags full of my clothes.
I knew what it all meant.

Don't let her leave me here, Daddy. . . .

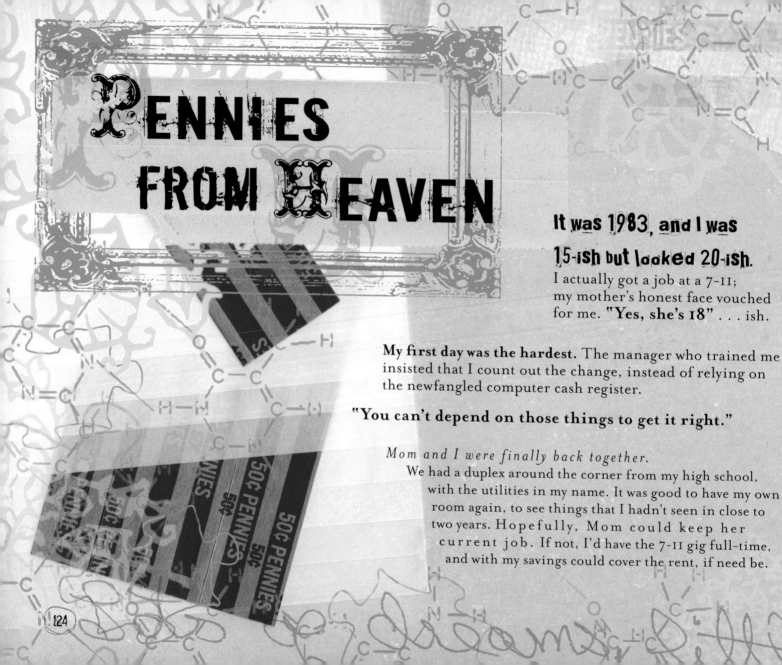

PENNIES FROM HEAVEN

It was 1983, and I was 15-ish but looked 20-ish. I actually got a job at a 7-11; my mother's honest face vouched for me. **"Yes, she's 18"** . . . ish.

My first day was the hardest. The manager who trained me insisted that I count out the change, instead of relying on the newfangled computer cash register.

"You can't depend on those things to get it right."

Mom and I were finally back together.
We had a duplex around the corner from my high school, with the utilities in my name. It was good to have my own room again, to see things that I hadn't seen in close to two years. Hopefully, Mom could keep her current job. If not, I'd have the 7-11 gig full-time, and with my savings could cover the rent, if need be.

I dont want you to be like me.

Lots of dreams, little substance.

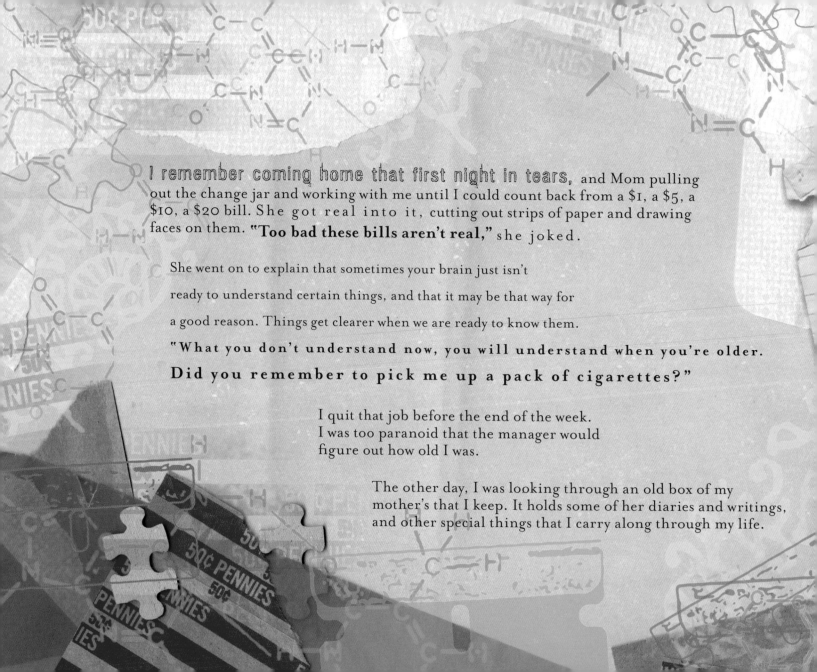

I remember coming home that first night in tears, and Mom pulling out the change jar and working with me until I could count back from a $1, a $5, a $10, a $20 bill. She got real into it, cutting out strips of paper and drawing faces on them. **"Too bad these bills aren't real,"** she joked.

She went on to explain that sometimes your brain just isn't

ready to understand certain things, and that it may be that way for

a good reason. Things get clearer when we are ready to know them.

"What you don't understand now, you will understand when you're older.

Did you remember to pick me up a pack of cigarettes?"

I quit that job before the end of the week.
I was too paranoid that the manager would
figure out how old I was.

The other day, I was looking through an old box of my
mother's that I keep. It holds some of her diaries and writings,
and other special things that I carry along through my life.

Love for David
by Celine

April 1968

I love you, not only for what you are
but for what I am when I am with you.
I love you, not only for what you have made of yourself
but for what you are making of me.
I love you for the part of me that you bring out
I love you for looking into my locked up heart
and drawing out into the light all the beautiful
thoughts that no one else had looked quite
far enough to find, and that even I didn't
know had there.

I love you for passing over all of my foolish
weak faults and accepting them instead of trying
to change them
I love you because you are helping me to make
out of the mess of my life, not a tavern, but a
temple; out of the works of my everyday life,
not a reproach, but a song
I love you because you have done more than
any parent could have done to make me good,
And more than any fate could have done to
make me happy.
You have done it without a touch, without
a word, without a sign.
You have done it by being yourself. Perhaps
that is what being a friend means after all!

I read and reread a particular poem—written to my Daddy. The page itself is so familiar to me—*her handwriting is like the curve of her cheekbone*—and now I finally get it.

It was dated 6 months before I was conceived. She was seeing both of them then. It could be a poem to either one—except she didn't write it. It's a poem called "Love," written by Roy Croft. *She just signed her name to it.*

Yeah, I get it now.
I understand.
    I can count back from
    that $2 bill.

Soon I will know.
I will know who I am.

THE RULES

The first rule was, I was not allowed to set foot in Paradise, CA. The second rule was, I was not allowed to ride in VW Bugs, but I'll get to that later.

I remember green hills and tall pine trees, and at the base of those green hills and tall pine trees were the leftovers of what was once a flat-topped shopping center. Rows—well, maybe a row—of stores, many closed, connected together like a grand display of boulders. There was a small video arcade with a boarded-up window, still open for business. Some bare-chested boys (away-from-home cute) were hanging out front in unbuttoned plaid shirts, riding pieced-together bicycles, eating slices of Paradise Pizza, though that shop looked closed, too. That was all there was to do there, it seemed—just hang out, forever.

"This is Paradise,"
my Mom introduced sarcastically.

Paradise, CA, a small town nestled in the foothills
of the Sierra Nevada Mountains. A town that looked
like gold miners came and went and came and went.
A place I'd promise my mother I'd never go to again.

**"God help us if we ever set foot in this
fucking hellhole after today,"** she said.

We had left home at about 4 in the morning to miss the traffic.
It was a somber drive from the bay to the foothills.

Every time I spoke, my Mom would turn the CB radio up a little louder. It
was a long drive. I started to count the number of cigarettes she juggled.
I watched in wonder at the way she drove and smoked and listened and talked
all at once.

**"Yeah, I'm going to pick her up now.
I'll drag her out of there if I have to. Over."**

Speak, smoke, drive,
speak, smoke, drive.

I'M NOT SURE HOW LONG IT HAD BEEN
since my brother Bob's bereavement leave had ended.
He was back at the army base in Washington
now, without his *teen bride* and without having
buried the remains of his firstborn, *a baby
boy*, declared dead in a delivery room at
Feather River Hospital not weeks before.
His bride's parents had insisted that she stay behind,
as if the marriage were ANNULLED BY THE TRAGEDY.

"Yeah, the coroner said there was blue in my grandson's lungs.
That means they didn't try hard enough to save him. OVER."

Hiss. Mumble. "Ten-four, he was alive.
I'm on my way to go get my daughter-in-law
and take her back to my son,
right where she belongs. OVER."

In the end, her parents were right:
The marriage didn't last. And with the money from the legal suit,
my brother's ex-wife built them a big red barn to make amends.
My Mom said my brother didn't see a red cent, or even the baby's headstone.

"They're gonna wake up one day and see that barn's been burned to a crisp!"

AS YEARS PASSED, my brother's tragedy became less his and
more my mother's, as if the act of his
b u r y i n g t h e p a s t in one way or another
gave her c u s t o d y r i g h t s.

She'd tell the story of how she dressed the baby's body in a soft

baby-blue layette, which she had crocheted for his homecoming.

She'd tell the story of how his spirit followed her home and stayed.

He slept in her room. *He sat on her
knee when she was sewing.* He ran up
and down our hallway and caused
sudden breezes, ELECTRICAL OUTAGES,
telephone hang-ups. She was the mother
of his **"earthbound soul."**

Then one day, like all her babies,

she left him behind, too.

robert 11/62

BABY #5

Once, my big brother had a proud dad.

Tall and strong.

And then—he didn't.

So the story goes.

"You don't stay with a man that beats you.
You get the hell outta there and you never go back.
You wait until he's sleeping—
you tie his arms and legs to the 4-poster bed—

you pack your bags and your lipstick and grab your wrought-iron frying pan
AND YOU BE SURE TO BREAK EVERY BONE IN HIS BODY."

Mother went west, back to the house with its arms full of crocheted blankets.
Bobby never saw his father again—
but a wrought-iron frying pan sat in the cabinet for years.

PROMENADE GIRL

*Allemande left
and a do–si–do
move your ex–con
around you go*
Pass thru the corner
2 and 4
Now wheel and deal her
thru the jail cell door
*Come on, circle left
and then you tip her—
Who knew! This shady lady was once a stripper!*

Mom took up singles' square dancing.
She got a lot of attention with the elaborate costumes
she would spend all night making on her sewing machine.

I eventually got used to the sound,
and was able to imagine the thickness of the fabric,
or if it was a hem or a pleat. The spinning of the motor
would stitch me into a b l a n k e t of *deep sleep*.

She had met a man with money.

He was worse than shy, lacking in social skills, a bit of a square, and eleven years her junior. They did the Right and Left Grand every Wednesday, and he came over every Sunday for dinner.

She'd marinate New York steaks in Italian salad dressing and sear them in the broiler, *"Sicilian style."* She'd make him Western shirts of gold lamé or sometimes silk, which m a t c h e d the bodices of her dresses. This claimed him on the floor—they were a pair. MY BIKER MAMA TURNED BETTY CROCKER. She kept her man well dressed and full of food . . . while she scraped together money for *crinolines*, and soft leather dance shoes.

She had a plan and it included holding out on sex—
AS WAS PROPER FOR A CORNER MAID.

Time was running out.
All those lines that my mother had sucked up her nose now began to show on her face.

I'd be 16 soon. My SSI death-benefit checks—the ones she had been collecting every month since David Crooks died—WERE GOING TO STOP. So far in her life, she hadn't been able to hold a job longer than 12 months. She needed money and *she just so happened to need love, too.*

SOCIAL SECURITY

THERE WAS NO SCRIPT.

There was no caller singing the turns.
I was simply raised to go along with whatever she said, OR . . . ELSE.

So with that—
we owned a home in the Central Valley
but lived in the Bay Area by choice,
MOM WAS A CERTIFIED PUBLIC ACCOUNTANT
her ex-boyfriend (the one who was renting
out the garage and paid me to iron his clothes)
was her brother,
and everything was normal and proper,
like overcooked steak and potatoes.

This dance landed her a diamond wedding
band and do-si-doed us to a house in the
hills. We even had a microwave.
But it wasn't easy getting there.

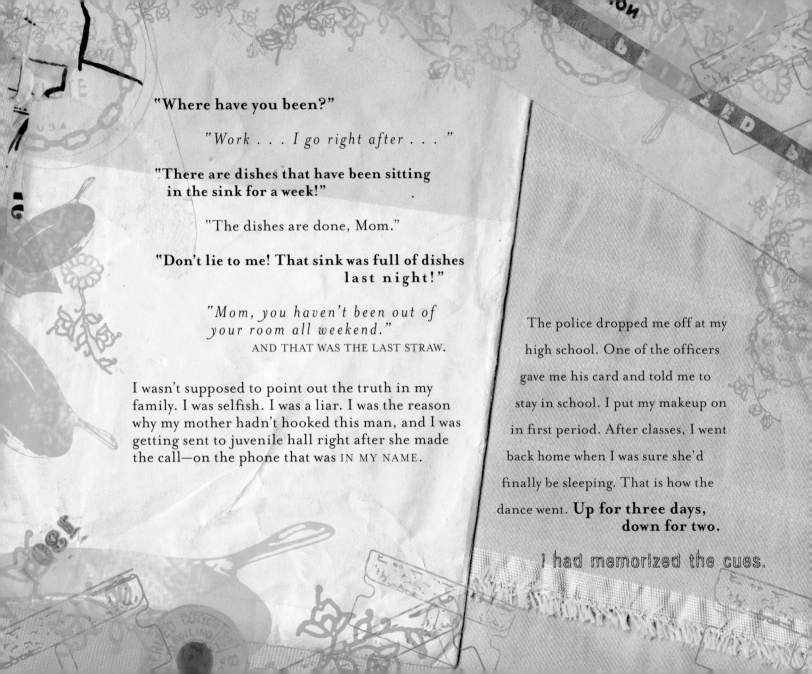

"Where have you been?"

"Work . . . I go right after . . . "

"There are dishes that have been sitting in the sink for a week!"

"The dishes are done, Mom."

"Don't lie to me! That sink was full of dishes last night!"

"Mom, you haven't been out of your room all weekend."
AND THAT WAS THE LAST STRAW.

I wasn't supposed to point out the truth in my family. I was selfish. I was a liar. I was the reason why my mother hadn't hooked this man, and I was getting sent to juvenile hall right after she made the call—on the phone that was IN MY NAME.

The police dropped me off at my high school. One of the officers gave me his card and told me to stay in school. I put my makeup on in first period. After classes, I went back home when I was sure she'd finally be sleeping. That is how the dance went. **Up for three days, down for two.**

I had memorized the cues.

REUNION PART 1

David Hans Schnabel called and said he's coming out to take the DNA test Saturday.

october 6, 2004

It makes me think of the last time I saw him— leaves were green, life was truth, and I was 17. I had just graduated high school—breaking a long-standing tradition. I wasn't *pregnant*. I had no babies. I w a s n ' t a n a d d i c t .

My mother and I never spoke of the **"Daddy"** issue after THAT DAY, 5 YEARS BEFORE—when she drove me around the block and dropped me off, *without a father or a home.*

That was a long time ago, and things had changed. A little.

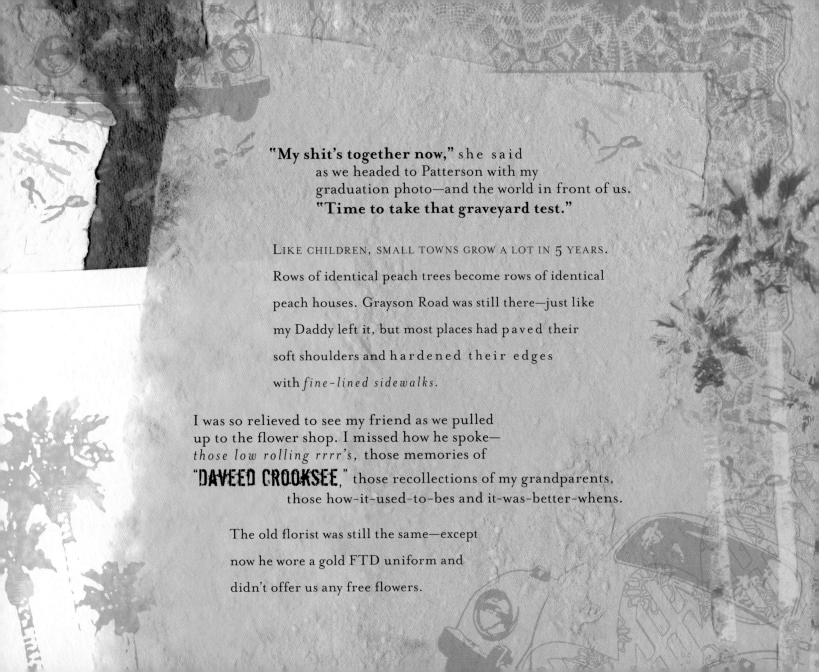

"My shit's together now," she said
as we headed to Patterson with my
graduation photo—and the world in front of us.
"Time to take that graveyard test."

LIKE CHILDREN, SMALL TOWNS GROW A LOT IN 5 YEARS.

Rows of identical peach trees become rows of identical

peach houses. Grayson Road was still there—just like

my Daddy left it, but most places had paved their

soft shoulders and hardened their edges

with *fine-lined sidewalks.*

I was so relieved to see my friend as we pulled
up to the flower shop. I missed how he spoke—
those low rolling rrrr's, those memories of
"DAVEED CROOKSEE," those recollections of my grandparents,
those how-it-used-to-bes and it-was-better-whens.

The old florist was still the same—except

now he wore a gold FTD uniform and

didn't offer us any free flowers.

GRAVEYARDS NEVER CHANGE.
They grow in body, but remain constant and silent.
They search for no new identity, but accept them.
They are what they are, always, row after row, hole
after hole, life after stone after life after stone.

Mom walked with me this time. She didn't remember
exactly where he was—*so I showed her the way.*

Walk carefully
(head down to show respect),
one foot gently after the other—
along the edges of graves
(never across them).
Don't walk through the flowers
(and don't take them).

His grave is the one before the dwarf
fruit tree (don't pick the leaves), where the
sunlight hits the watered grass just so—
  it looks like someone
    spilled drops of glitter.
There's my Daddy.

"I bought that headstone, you know," she said, motioning toward his grave, about 9 feet away from where she had stopped.

"Your Grandma Crooks had the stone ordered and finished, but last minute I paid the carver extra to put that line on it." She read the inscription out loud:

"Let God light my way to Heaven."

We stood there for a moment. Quiet.

"I'm going to go have a cigarette."

"Okay, Mom."

I walked over and kneeled. I checked him for dirt and cracks. *I'm sorry it's been so long.* I put the flowers I had bought in the cement vase. I stuck my graduation photo and announcement into the gap between his headstone and the manicured earth. This was the first time I'd been to my DADDY'S grave since I'd found out about *David Hans Schnabel*.

**"I did it, Daddy. I'm the first one.
I graduated and I'm starting college soon."**
He knows I'm lying. *He knows I know.*

I fingered the grass like hair; I touched the pebbles like knuckles.
I looked up and around at the other graves, birth and death, and name
after name. I couldn't look him in the face. I found myself
counting the years of life, and grieving the loss of time. She was 75,
he was 74, my father was 26. SHE LIES, but she has a good heart, Daddy.

"I . . . I might not be your daughter."

When I got back to the car, Mom was sitting inside. She took her
compact mirror off my seat, wiped her nose, and then began
to drive out across the gravel and onto Highway 33. This part of
town had been left the same, *but I was leaving it changed.*

With one hand on the wheel, my Mom reached back
in her purse and pulled out her soft pack and lighter.

"So . . . do you wanna go see David Schnabel?"

REUNION
PART 2

My Mom stood inside a glass phone booth at an interstate truck stop.

She was calling him. Smoke was swirling and twirling up and off her fingertips—forming nimbus clouds that I thought might rain and rain. I stayed in the car—not wanting to lose the front seat to my guilt. *I'm sorry, Daddy.*

I STOOD THERE WITH MY MOM, on the welcome mat at *David Hans Schnabel's* doorstep, 18 years ago.

HE OPENED THE DOOR, WE WALKED IN, WE SAT IN THE KITCHEN AT A TABLE BY A WINDOW.

Who's gonna say it?

He talked about his bad back and his wife—
who wouldn't come out of her bedroom.

I know my Mom will say it.
He tells me now that he was waiting for my Mom to say
something.

Mom pulled another graduation photo from her monogrammed

purse and gave it to him. He pulled out his wallet. He put the photo in.

He then showed us a photo of one of his daughters, who was younger

than me. *We shouldn't be here.* My Mom asked about his wife.

"Why doesn't she come out to meet us?"
                    No one talks about who I am.
                    No one talks about my knowing the truth.

He says, **"She's not feeling well. She's, uh, sick."**

I don't remember anything else.

"Your Mom got real pissed! She said, 'Sick, huh? Does she
think she's too good for us?' Your Mom got up outta her seat
and marched down the hall and began pounding on all the doors,
yelling for her to come out. Saying she was gonna kick her ass. She
was a real spitfire, your mother!"

I DON'T REMEMBER THIS. I DON'T EVEN REMEMBER LEAVING.
I JUST REMEMBER FEELING SHAME.

"Yeah, she was a hellion, all right! She sure told me off! She said it
would be a cold day in hell before she'd come by again. She said
I'd have to be the one who called."
He trailed off a bit. **"Yeah . . . that CeAnne."**

YEAH, THAT CEANNE.
Out the door with a trail of smoke behind her.

"Well, Cori honey, I still have that graduation photo,
you know— I've kept it in my wallet this whole time."

"So . . . you think I might be your daughter?"

"Well," he paused again. "Why don't we
go ahead and take that test to be sure?"

A Nominative Case

He didn't show.

My gut knew.

There's not hurt or letdown—I mean, we're talking about a guy who had an idea that a kid might be his—and bailed.

Not quite an upstanding citizen or anything like that. I figured going into it that I was going to be meeting *some fella* who was *wrapped up in my Mom's past.*

I don't think there's a chance to find any winners.

I called Carla to confirm, and she answered her "I dunnos" in a groggy voice. She said she thought he might be working. She said she'd give him a call and call me back. She didn't.

Everything she said came and went, and I found myself back at the beginning.

146

I HATE YOUR ANSWERING MACHINE

a week later . . . .

BEEP.

"Hi Cori, it's Carla," she said.

"My Dad wanted to apologize,"
said Mr. Paternity Test in the background.

"Yeah, my Dad wanted to apologize for not making it last week; he was working."

"Mumble, mumble, mumble. . . ."

"What? . . . He says he went to sleep Saturday and didn't wake up till Sunday afternoon. Anyway, we were just calling to say hi."

"Mumble, mumble, and Carla is making apple pies."

**"Yeah, we have about 10 crusts and a
bushel of apples, and, uh . . .
I'm peeling them and making apple pie."**

"She's so full of shit, her eyes are brown."

PAUSE.

**"Anyway, um . . . give us a call back.
The number is xxx-xxxx."**

"Mumble, mumble."

"I dunno, Dad . . . say something!"

PAUSE. MUFFLE. PAUSE.

"How ya doing, Sister!"

"PPPfffttt . . .* Sister??? *Fffff." CLICK.

BEEP. BEEP.

RULE #2:
THE VW BUG

When you grow up with a liar, it takes a while before you understand what a lie really is.

THERE ARE ONLY TWO WAYS UP TO THE HOUSE ON THE HILL.

One is along the grassy backside of the high school, the 92 bus route, actually. A steep grade as far as suburbs in the EAST BAY go; make a right at the boys' home on the corner at the top. There's a mini-billboard in the yard. You'll know what I'm talking about when you see it.

The other way is up the main hill. It's a straight shot. No big twists or turns. Technically, it's the entrance to the college, but the locals never go that way. Pass the row of '80s luxury apartments with a mini-billboard marking the driveway; follow past as the road bends, and there's a stop sign at the top. MAKE A LEFT.

MY BIG CONCERN AT THAT VERY MOMENT was
which route she was going to take. It was usual for my Mom to
drive up the back road. No sidewalks. Houses with lots in between.
Dewy grass, and chicken fences.
The route reminded her that she'd made it to the hills.
(The long way up.)

No, no, no—my Mom had a habit of getting

a chicken supreme and a double-fudge cake

on the way home. Yes, it was more likely that

she would drive the extra mile along Mission

Boulevard to the college road. I nodded.

FUCK.

THEN, AFTER THAT, THERE'S A PERIOD OF
TIME WHEN YOU UNDERSTAND THAT THE LIAR
JUST WANTS PEOPLE TO LOVE HER.
WHAT A GLITCH! NO ONE EVER
REALLY KNOWS YOU WHEN YOU LIE.
SO THEY CAN'T EVER REALLY
LOVE YOU FOR REAL.

All of this map talk was fine and dandy, but there was no way I could explain the real trouble to my coworker. No way I could explain that my mother had "psychic powers." Oh, and that she had a vision I was going to die in a car like his, just like my father did—um, but he might not be my father. No way to tell him that I took a ride not because I thought he was cute, but because I needed to prove something to myself. Well, the stronger part of me had something to prove. The other part of me was kicking myself for not going up the back way. The other part of me was freaking out and needed to get the fuck off the hill 'cause if she found me in his car, she would kick my ass—oh, and probably his too. Back and forth, round and round, swinging all the while. There he goes, walking down the hill to the payphone at the car wash. I stayed behind, sitting on the divider that separated the tos from the fros on college hill, next to his very conspicuous and very stuck VW Bug.

THEN YOU GOT TO EXAMINE YOURSELF AND WHY YOU LIE . . . IS IT JUST LEARNED BEHAVIOR? OR ARE YOU AFRAID OF BEING CLOSE TO PEOPLE TOO? MAYBE ALL ALONG, MY MOM'S WAY OF LOVING ME WAS TEACHING ME HOW TO NEVER KNOW LOVE.

I needed to stop lying, and I think my first step was to stop living lies.

When Steve first asked if I needed a ride home from work that day, I had forgotten he drove a Bug. I SWEAR. Maybe. It wasn't until we got out to the parking lot that I realized it. *Okay, yeah, I knew.* But I didn't really know. **Yes, I did.**

THIS WAS ALL RIGHT AROUND THE TIME WHEN I WAS STARTING TO GET THAT MY MOM WAS *NUTS*.

Well, no, I always knew, but what I mean is, what you know seems to get a lot clearer the longer you know it, sometimes. She was sick and I could see it spreading. Crazy people don't just stop becoming crazy. *They get more and more crazy until they're so full of crazy that they have to start doling it out and have others be crazy for them.*

Anyway, this time I knew I needed to step out and separate my self from what there was of her in me.

I needed to put the crazy down, right there beside the VW Bug.

SO I GOT INTO HIS CAR. **Inside. Inside. Inside.**
I was overwhelmed with the thought that these were my last moments.
Tick, tick, tick. I've lived my mother's lies for far too long. They've become my truth.
On my last day alive, I wore a red sweater. I took a deep breath.
Don't let her bat with your head. I tried to act normal.
This is not going to kill me. **"Hey, Steve. Nice car."**

SO THIS IS WHAT IT LOOKED LIKE. This was the last of what my

DADDY saw before his head crushed in and he became a vegetable.

I had never in my life, aside from a Herbie movie, seen the inside
of one of these cars. The roof was like delicate paper, the dashboard,
molded papier-mâché. Cellophane windows and crepe paper wheels;
the door just slits, to stuff birthday candy inside.
This sweater is itchy. **My Daddy died in a piñata.**

Somewhere in me was the voice that had always

been there. Maybe it's the voice that speaks

today. My fate was not my father's. My story

would not be the lies my mother told me.

I was going to be okay. I can pull the

blindfold down now. I am almost there.

DIARY

So back on the guardrail, when I saw my
mother's car at the bottom of the hill,
I knew that I just might be able to face her.
The time had come.

What would I say?
I wasn't going to lie this time. I wasn't going to lie anymore.
I would tell her that I wasn't going to die in a damned
VW Bug—and she knew that. I'd tell her I could see her
for who she really was. I knew all the lies and all the scams, and
no matter how often she denied it,
I knew she was still on crank.

I'd tell her that despite it all, I still loved her.

She didn't see me standing in the middle of the road.
She was looking forward with her cigarette lighting the way,
and the conversation in her head was so out loud that it
sounded like she was saying something to me.

I SAW HER PASS.

Hmm—sometimes I didn't love her.
Sometimes she wasn't my mother.
Sometimes she was just a stranger.

She nodded her head and took a large

bite of her chicken sandwich.

CINDY'S HAIR was as blond as the silk pulled from sweet god corn, harvested on cloudy angel farms. It made her eyes look bluer than the gray-blue of our mother's blues.

cynthia 1/65

156

BABY #6

"You could sit her right next to those dolls and not be able to pick her out."

But you could. Cindy was the heavenly one.

SOMETIMES THE HOUSE CREAKS.
Her floors are old but refuse the silence of age.
Her vision has left, and her voice has dropped further back, but still her memories
float like broken, swaying chandeliers—shedding small fragments of colored light,
here and . . .

. . . and there—a messenger!
BOBBY AND CINDY HAVE THE SAME FATHER.
No, the twins' father came back around the same time Charlotte got pregnant with Cindy.

NO, CHARLOTTE SLEPT WITH AUNT KELLY'S HUSBAND.
CINDY AND COUSIN ERIC ARE BROTHER AND SISTER.

NO. NO. NO.
Zeus, taking the form of a Hells Angel, rode past that house
and lifted Charlotte up off the sidewalk and onto his thighs.
He gunned his pistons and cycled his cylinders
and drove through her tunnels and shot past her barriers—
until he shifted to a lower gear, where he laid her down,
soft and pregnant—on the lap of my great-grandmother's house.

Declining the Crown

So I called Carla back.

"You know, um . . .
What you said about hoping your Dad
doesn't love me more than he loves you . . .
those words stuck with me. I'm worried that you
think I want more than I do. I want you to know
that I only want the answer to the paternity test—
and nothing else."

JUST DON'T ASK ME WHY I WANT IT—
BECAUSE I'M NOT SURE ANYMORE.

Silence.

"**Carla—I've been without parents for a very long time now. I'm not looking for new ones.** If the test is positive, your Dad won't be anything more to me than what he is now—my mother's old friend." I think.

She finally spoke.

"**Oh—I know, I'm sorry I said that. It was something I felt, but it went away once I said it.** If the test is positive and you're my sister, then you are family and you're not going to get rid of me that easily. In fact, I hope you are my sister! I really do!"

Silence.
"**Don't you?**" she asked.
It's hard, Carla.

She said that there was a big something to tell me.

Did I remember how she said Kimmy had come down last summer

to see her graduate from some sort of program? I'd never asked

the details about it because I'd had a sinking feeling.

"I graduated from a drug-rehab program."

Here I am again. Sitting here, knowing before the know. Everything starts to spin, and I see the same old faces and hear those familiar scattered tones of voice that gurgle in the black twirling pools. I can't help but make a mental count of all those people in my life who were ruined. All those people whose faces were scarred from the picking, whose teeth were worn from the grinding, whose jaws seemed to move freely after they finished speaking, whose eyes were black and endlessly awake and ready for just one more line—yeah, just one more and then I'll come down, and then I'll sleep and get straight—I promise.

"Wow. That's really great, Carla. Congratulations. It's a big deal." It's amazing what you can say when a whirlpool begins to swirl.

"Well," she hesitates.
SO YOU'RE GONNA SAY YOU'RE USING AGAIN, RIGHT?
"My life is still pretty messed up."

Swirling and knowing.

I went on to ask what drug, when I knew. *CRANK*.
I went on to ask if she was clean, when I knew. *NO*.
I went on to ask if she was using right then, when I knew, when I didn't want to know. *YES*.

Back in '93, I got a call from my Mom's dealer.

The one who'd found her soaking dead
in our bathtub just two years earlier.
She told me Cindy had been picked up with an 8-ball of
crank down the street from my Great-Grandma's house and
hauled off to Santa Rita. She needed me to go to the kids.

I don't remember the lie I told her babies, but I do remember how
I felt like it was all happening again. History was repeating itself—
and if something didn't happen, one of Cindy's babies
would come home from identifying her body at the hospital,
and be left with the task of draining the tub of her death water.

A few days later, after she was released, I went by to
pick her up for her hearing. SHE WAS HIGH AS A BUOY.
Her eyes were black, her sentences struggling to stay afloat.

"The judge is going to know, Cindy."

Gurgle, gurgle, spurt.

I hoped for a second that I might float away and break free of her.

In the end she was given probation because it was a first offense. And when the judge ordered her to test that day, there was no one in the probation office to do it. She was given a date to report back on.

TWEAKER'S LUCK.

I wish I could say that my sister got clean, and that I was able to help her. I wish I could say that I would go to her house on rainy evenings to watch the kids while she faithfully went to NA meetings.

I wish I could say that in the following year, she didn't take the power of attorney over our GREAT-GRANDMOTHER *and use it to refinance the house, put her in a rest home, and then blow the money on chicken scratch.*

And one baby-sitting weekend,
when she didn't come back
for her babies,
I KNEW I'D LOST HER.
I'd lost my sister like I lost my mother.
When she finally came home,
I kissed her babies for the last time,
called her on her shit,
and that was the end of us.

She set me free.

**"I just wanted to be completely
honest with you,"** Carla struggled.

I KNOW.

"I betcha don't wanna take that test now—"

"No, Carla, I want to take the test."

**"Well, if you don't mind not mentioning this to my
father, because he doesn't know I'm using again. . . . "**

More lies.

GIRL TROUBLE 1

The second time my Mom faked cancer

was an elaborate, last-ditch attempt to keep her marriage together.

SHE SHAVED HER HEAD AND STOPPED WEARING HER DENTURES. She said she had to drive all the way out to Stanford University, an hour and a half round trip, for her treatments. She was taking part in a new study, involving lasers. It would cost nothing. On the days when she was scheduled to go under the beam, she would be gone only the better part of an hour. *She'd come home with her arms full of shopping bags.* When I questioned her, she would show me bare spots on her scalp.

I found a pink Lady Bic shaver, clogged with her hair, stuffed under the cushions of the couch where she slept.

She and her husband, after 1 year of marriage, no longer shared a bed, AND THERE WAS A LITTLE MATTER OF

some missing money. . . .

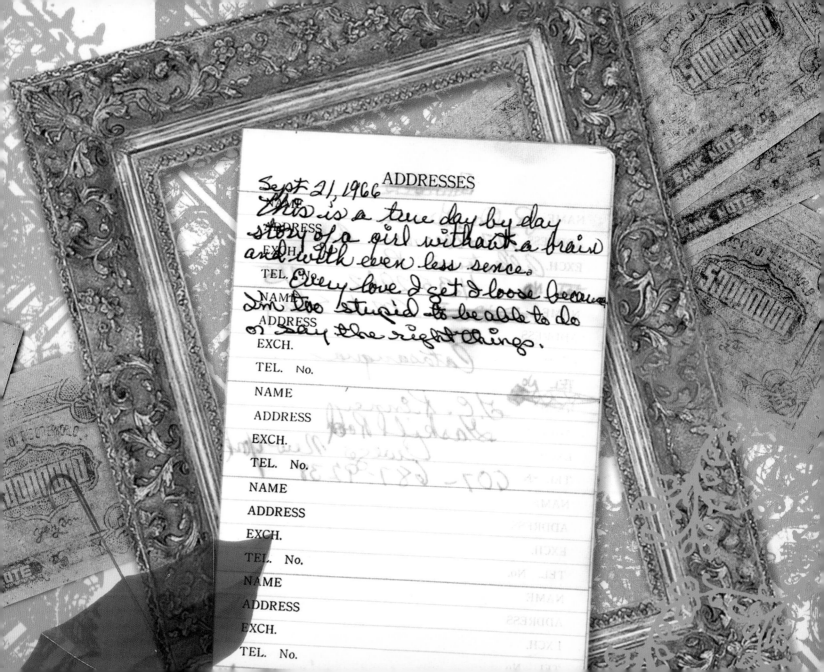

ADDRESSES

Sept 21, 1966

This is a true day by day story of a girl without a brain and with even less sence. Every love I get I loose because I'm too stupid to be able to do or say the right things.

Love, Soft as an Easy Chair

When I was 10, I pulled off my second big lie.

I had one of those movie-star address books, the kind that you pay $3 for at a tourist shop. It said, "Visit the Stars!" on the cover. *I imagined doing just that.*

I wrote a letter to Matthew Laborteaux. He was that orphan the Ingalls family adopted on a visit to the "big city." He brought life back to *Little House on the Prairie* after Nellie started to get all nice.

I wrote him and asked if he and his brother wanted to go on a date with me and my best friend, "Stormy."

(We called each other by our pretend horse names.)

Stormy had moved away more than a year before, but we still kept in touch. I thought it'd be a great way to get to see her again, meet two cute TV-star boys, and gallop away into the sunset.

I also wrote Barbra Streisand.
My Mom loved Barbra Streisand.
After the movie A STAR IS BORN came out on HBO,
my Mom got one of those home perm kits and did her
hair to look just like Esther Hoffman's. The house stunk
real bad, but she looked SO PRETTY. I wrote Barbra and
told her my Mom was dying of a *rare and insufferable
disease.* I said that she could die any day now.
I asked if she could send a picture signed,

To my twin and biggest fan, CeAnna!
Your friend,
Barbra Streisand

I wondered if she would know I was lying
because I didn't ask her to say, "Get well."

About a year later—and, oddly, about one week apart—

I received envelopes from Matthew Laborteaux and from

Barbra Streisand. Both envelopes contained glossy, mass-

printed, 8x10 photos. Mathew didn't respond about the

double date, and Barbra's photo had only an autograph,

but it was fine by me. My Mom was very happy when I gave

her the picture. Sometimes she would look at it when using

her hair pick, to get her perm just so.

GIRL TROUBLE 2

facades hold up only so long.
glass-half-empty clouds.
sooner or later someone's
gonna figure you out.
they're gonna see you slosh and break—
they will see what you really are, or
you're gonna spill.
you are going to spill
to save yourself—
take my yellow raincoat.

They co-owned a Union 76. She and he, with them. *It was his dream.*
We went to late dinners over at the Chows' house. Playing husband, wife,
and daughter. It was a house much HIGHER IN THE HILLS than ours.
We sat in the family room with all the men, who drank and sang karaoke
with the television, in their starched shirts and loosened ties.

"Take out your nose ring," she'd say to me quietly
while he boasted! While she dispensed compliments!
I completed the picture.

Four sweaty hundred dollars—that's all there was!
I reached my hand into the bank bag and pulled
out 3 wads of cash, wrapped in deposit slips that
were written in my mother's handwriting and
secured with pink rubber bands.

THE CHOWS WERE IMPRESSED WITH HER.
"A woman of intelligence," someone said, nodding.

It wasn't long before she was put in charge of the
accounting and taxes. She put a high heel to the
pedal whenever she went into that little office beside
the restroom. She made the men in the shop feel
IMPORTANT. They liked how she'd wink when she
joked about Ben Wa balls and pinky-size pricks.

Her hands smelled like gasoline.
She revved their engines.

Four stinky hundred dollars!
  When we got home, I went to my room and stuck the
  money in the toe of a Payless ShoeSource cowboy boot.
  I didn't count the money until months later.

MOM SAID SHE NEEDED TO TALK. She said money had come up missing at
the gas station, and the partnership with the Chow family was dissolving. Her
square-dancing husband was sure to lose a lot of money, and because my mother
was in charge of the deposits, she was the suspect.

Four horrible hundred dollars!
  "It's okay, Mom, I'll stay in the car and watch
  the deposit. You can run into the store—no prob."

Her eyes were so dilated. I was so sick of the blacks of her eyes.
Black eyes never see you. *Black eyes never suspect you.*
  Black eyes soak in exclusive pools, alone.

GOOD GIRL.

She told me that the Chows had hired a private detective who was
bound to do a background check on her. We sat quietly for a while.

Then I asked her,
"How much money is missing?"

"Almost $15,000."

       Almost $15,000? But I stole $400.
       I counted it, and it was only $400. I was a chump.

**"You can tell him the truth, Mom—just tell him the truth.
About everything, Mom. He loves you, and it will be okay."**

Those were the last words I said to her that day. Those were the last

words I said before she looked at me, before she took a drag off her

cigarette, before she soaked me with the **REAL TRUTH**. . . .

ALTAMONT

David Hans Schnabel said that one time my Mom had gotten my Aunt Kelly to watch us kids so he could take her out on a real date. When he pulled up, my aunt hopped into the front seat of his car and said she was going instead. *David Hans Schnabel* said he didn't mind, 'cause she was a real looker.

"Just when I started up the car, your Mom came running out of the apartment and pulled your aunt off the front seat by her red hair! She would have kicked her ass if we weren't late for the concert," he reminisced.

"What concert?" I asked.

"Altamont."

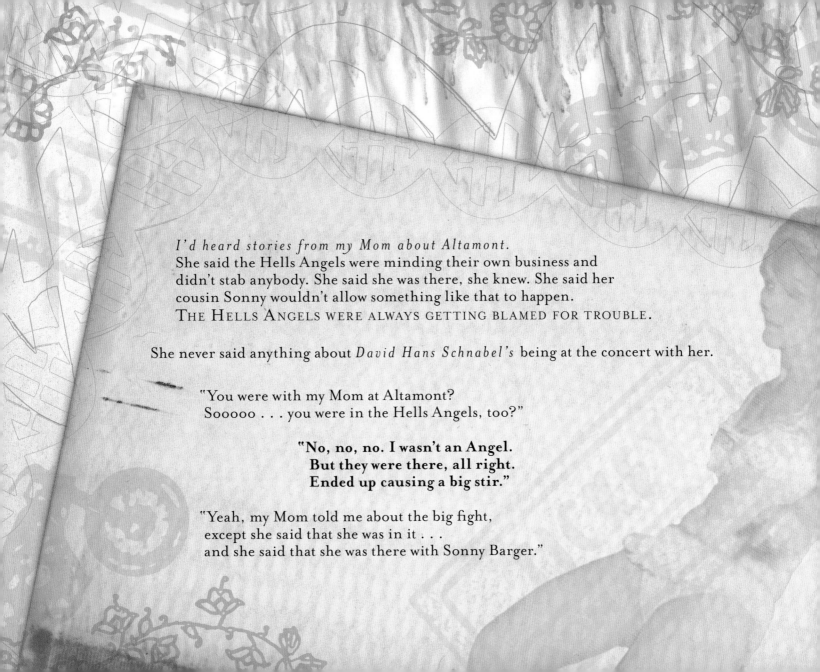

I'd heard stories from my Mom about Altamont.
She said the Hells Angels were minding their own business and
didn't stab anybody. She said she was there, she knew. She said her
cousin Sonny wouldn't allow something like that to happen.
THE HELLS ANGELS WERE ALWAYS GETTING BLAMED FOR TROUBLE.

She never said anything about *David Hans Schnabel's* being at the concert with her.

    "You were with my Mom at Altamont?
    Sooooo . . . you were in the Hells Angels, too?"

        "No, no, no. I wasn't an Angel.
        But they were there, all right.
        Ended up causing a big stir."

    "Yeah, my Mom told me about the big fight,
      except she said that she was in it . . .
      and she said that she was there with Sonny Barger."

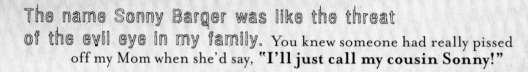

The name Sonny Barger was like the threat
of the evil eye in my family. You knew someone had really pissed
off my Mom when she'd say, **"I'll just call my cousin Sonny!"**

Except there was no cousin Sonny.

"No, no, no. We left before the Rolling Stones,
before the big fight. We both had to work early in the morning . . .
I don't remember seeing her cousin," he said.

"Ah . . . she was telling you he was her cousin, too?
She was bullshitting," I said.

"You got that right? Well, how about that!" He paused.
"Well, if he wasn't her cousin, then they were real good friends."

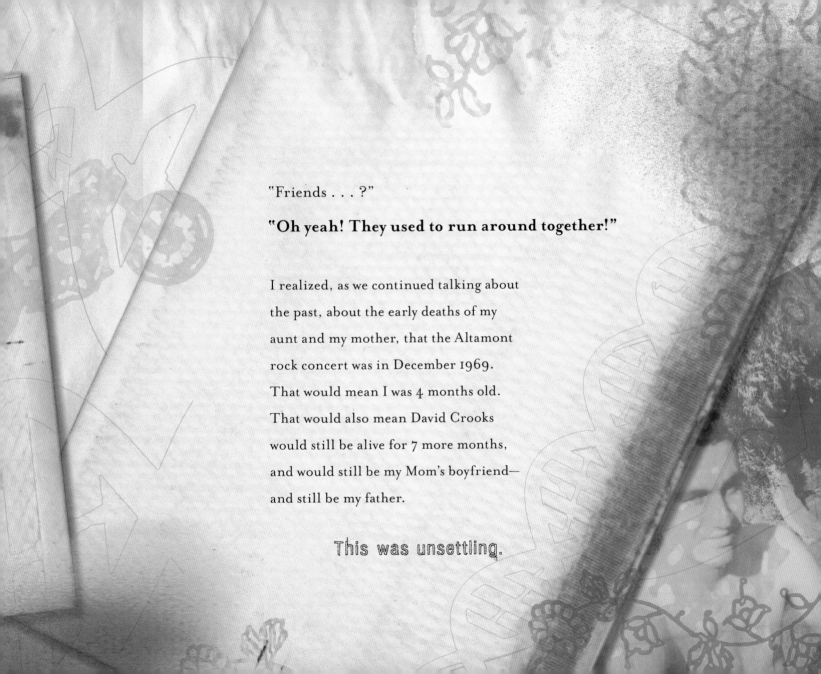

"Friends . . . ?"

"Oh yeah! They used to run around together!"

I realized, as we continued talking about
the past, about the early deaths of my
aunt and my mother, that the Altamont
rock concert was in December 1969.
That would mean I was 4 months old.
That would also mean David Crooks
would still be alive for 7 more months,
and would still be my Mom's boyfriend—
and still be my father.

This was unsettling.

GIRL TROUBLE 3

We sat outside ourselves.
Two figures watching
and listening.
No.
Not quite listening.
Far away from mother,
far away from daughter,
that was how we met—
that was how she told me.

A Florida swamp,
A car that wouldn't sink,
and some snapshots of a little trouble girl.

GIRLS LOVE TO BE TOLD THEY'RE PRETTY.

He liked how she'd get a thrill when he'd knock over
a gas station, and that sassy way she'd speak up to the
motel man's questions: **"Yes, we're married!"**

He'd let her drive when it was early—when the sun was rising
and the cops were sleeping. She'd step on the clutch and he'd
do the shifting. She'd smile that big smile, the one
that covered her face like a DIRTY KISS—
this girl's not afraid of nothin'.

Before long, she'd have that car wired and running

for him as he fled the scene. As he pulled her panty

hose off his face, he'd run to catch the open door—

time after time along the East Coast roads that

wound their way down to his money in Florida.

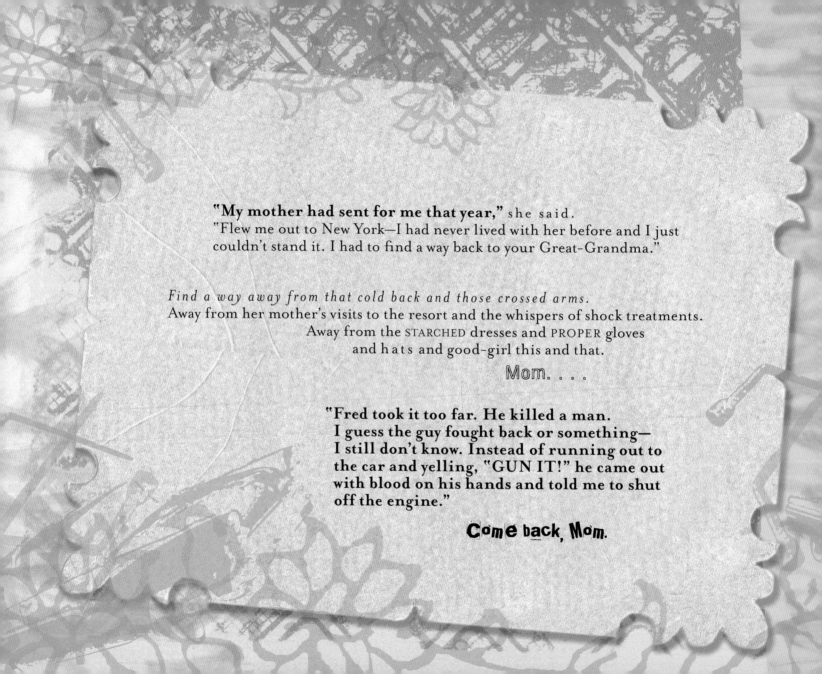

"My mother had sent for me that year," she said.
"Flew me out to New York—I had never lived with her before and I just
couldn't stand it. I had to find a way back to your Great-Grandma."

Find a way away from that cold back and those crossed arms.
Away from her mother's visits to the resort and the whispers of shock treatments.
Away from the STARCHED dresses and PROPER gloves
and h a t s and good-girl this and that.

Mom. . . .

**"Fred took it too far. He killed a man.
I guess the guy fought back or something—
I still don't know. Instead of running out to
the car and yelling, "GUN IT!" he came out
with blood on his hands and told me to shut
off the engine."**

Come back, Mom.

CALENDAR DISC
LIFT UP HERE

THE OTHER BROTHERS

The last time I spoke with Dennis

was long before I found David Schnabel. Dennis was talking about how nice it would be to drive his '65 Chevy on the windy roads of the California coast. He spends his time away from the grocery store restoring old cars and fixing neighborhood bicycles. He says that his wife and kids have never seen the ocean. He talked about how it's been too long since he saw me last, or since he paid a visit to our father's grave.

My big brothers, Dennis and Ron, haven't lived in California since after our dad died. Their mom got as far away as she could— *from the love she lost twice and the best friend who took him, my Mom.*

THEY BECAME TRAVELERS—LIVED ON THE ROAD, CAMPED, SAW THE COUNTRY. They slept in tepees and visited nudist colonies. *They were taught to hunt and fish and have a healthy disrespect for authority.* They settled in Colorado first—that's where my brothers found wives, who would teach them to read. They then bought land in Missouri and built three houses.

Dear brother
Grandma Crooks gave
me your address please
write to me too I am
sending your my picture
I am seven years old
and in the second grade
can you please send
me you picture I LOVE YOU
both VERY much,

your sister

Corina Crooks

Cori Crooks
344 Sunset B
Hayward, C

Cori

Cori
G

RETURNED
TO
SENDER
ADDRESSEE

, Neveda 89503

NOT AT THIS ADDRESS

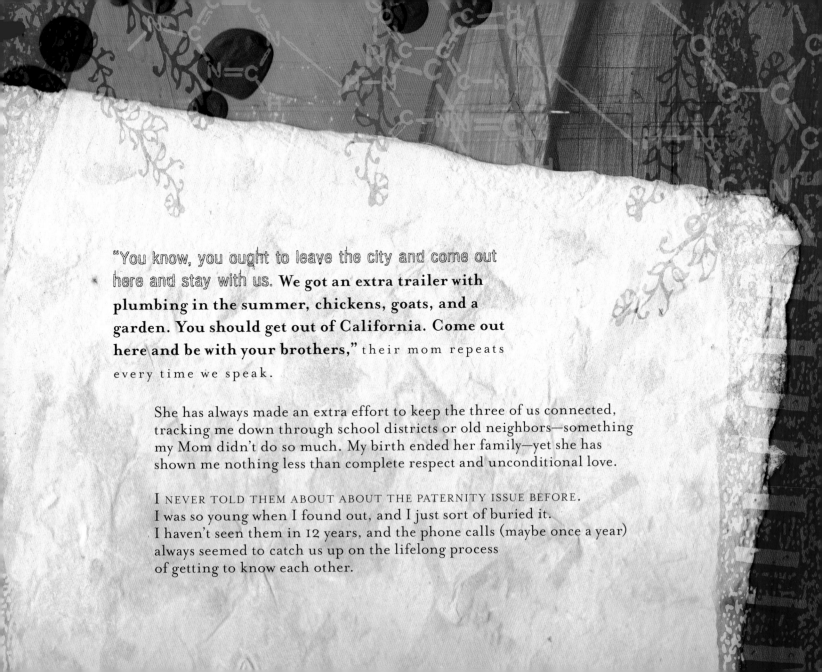

"You know, you ought to leave the city and come out here and stay with us. **We got an extra trailer with plumbing in the summer, chickens, goats, and a garden. You should get out of California. Come out here and be with your brothers,"** their mom repeats every time we speak.

She has always made an extra effort to keep the three of us connected, tracking me down through school districts or old neighbors—something my Mom didn't do so much. My birth ended her family—yet she has shown me nothing less than complete respect and unconditional love.

I NEVER TOLD THEM ABOUT ABOUT THE PATERNITY ISSUE BEFORE. I was so young when I found out, and I just sort of buried it. I haven't seen them in 12 years, and the phone calls (maybe once a year) always seemed to catch us up on the lifelong process of getting to know each other.

DEAR DIARY

Last night I inserted the CATCH ALL™ samples in the appropriately labeled tubes and reassembled them after allowing the swabs to dry at room temperature for two hours. I attached the corresponding *Tamper Seal* firmly over the area where the tube portions meet. I ensured that the *Tamper Seal* was visible: numbers 24 and 25 for CROOKS/CHILD, numbers 26 and 27 for SCHNABEL/SUSPECTED FATHER.

I SAW FIGURE 5.
I repeated steps when necessary.

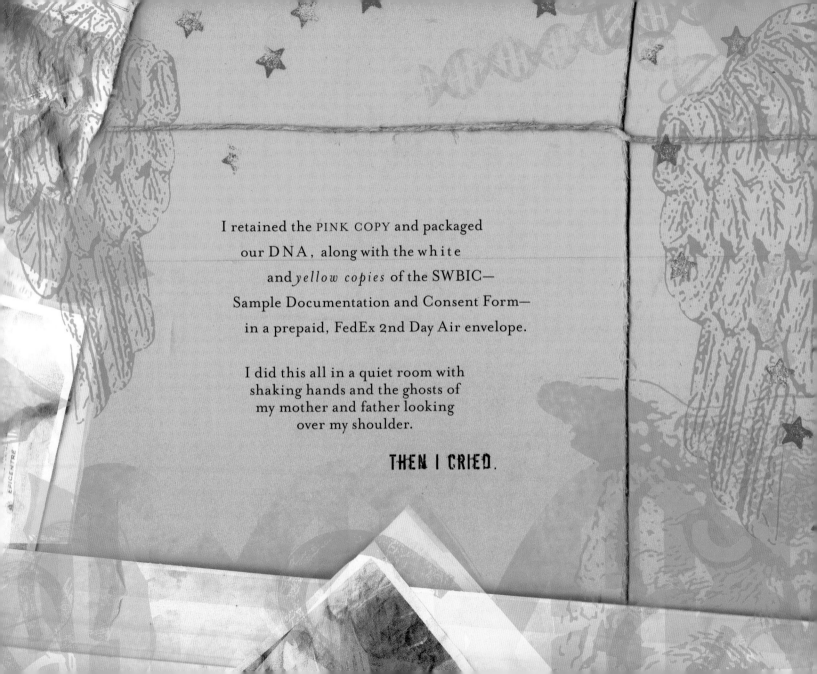

I retained the PINK COPY and packaged
our DNA, along with the white
and *yellow copies* of the SWBIC—
Sample Documentation and Consent Form—
in a prepaid, FedEx 2nd Day Air envelope.

I did this all in a quiet room with
shaking hands and the ghosts of
my mother and father looking
over my shoulder.

THEN I CRIED.

GIRL TROUBLE 4

My Mother carried the legs of the dead gas-station attendant.

She did everything Fred said. She moved a little to the right, *she walked quicker,* she turned her face away while Fred rifled through the pockets for keys to the only other vehicle on the lot besides theirs.

"You're not gonna get all scared on me, are you?"

They pulled the dead body onto the back seat and shut the doors after a few attempts; they had to reposition his knees. Fred had a wild look, like a barbed-wire tumbleweed, like he thought she had an escape plan.

"You're going to drive the body," he said.

He said that she was acting like she didn't love him. *She didn't.* He said she was acting like she was gonna run off. *She would.*

He said that they were gonna find a place to ditch the car and the body and she wasn't gonna leave him on his own to do it, and if she thought of cutting out, she'd have a whole mess of explaining to do with a dead man as a passenger.

"Aren't you glad you learned to drive?" he laughed.

SHE DID EVERYTHING FRED SAID. She signaled when he signaled. She followed close behind, down two-lane roads and across deltas filled with murky water, transporting the body of a man just a few years older than she was.

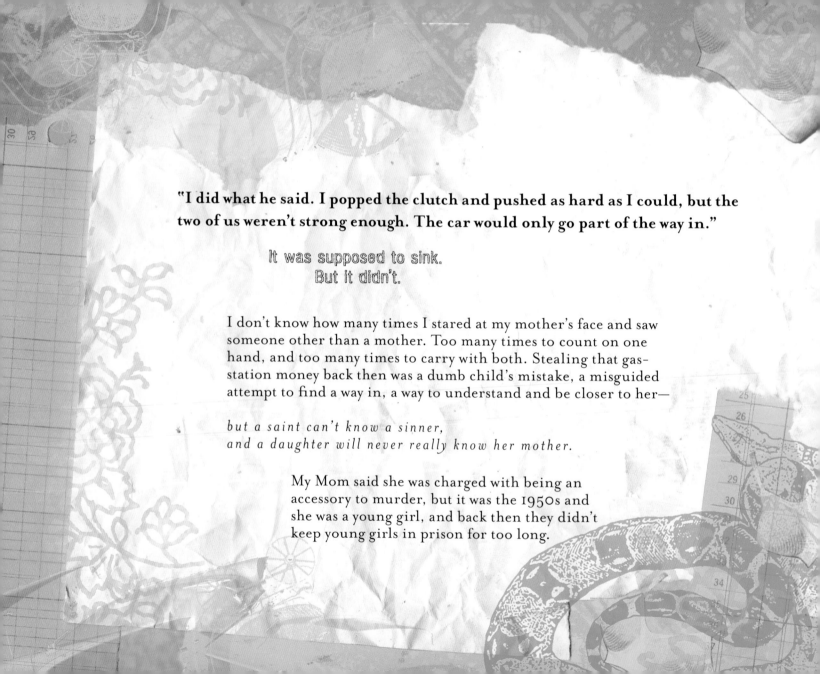

"I did what he said. I popped the clutch and pushed as hard as I could, but the two of us weren't strong enough. The car would only go part of the way in."

It was supposed to sink.
But it didn't.

I don't know how many times I stared at my mother's face and saw someone other than a mother. Too many times to count on one hand, and too many times to carry with both. Stealing that gas-station money back then was a dumb child's mistake, a misguided attempt to find a way in, a way to understand and be closer to her—

but a saint can't know a sinner,
and a daughter will never really know her mother.

My Mom said she was charged with being an accessory to murder, but it was the 1950s and she was a young girl, and back then they didn't keep young girls in prison for too long.

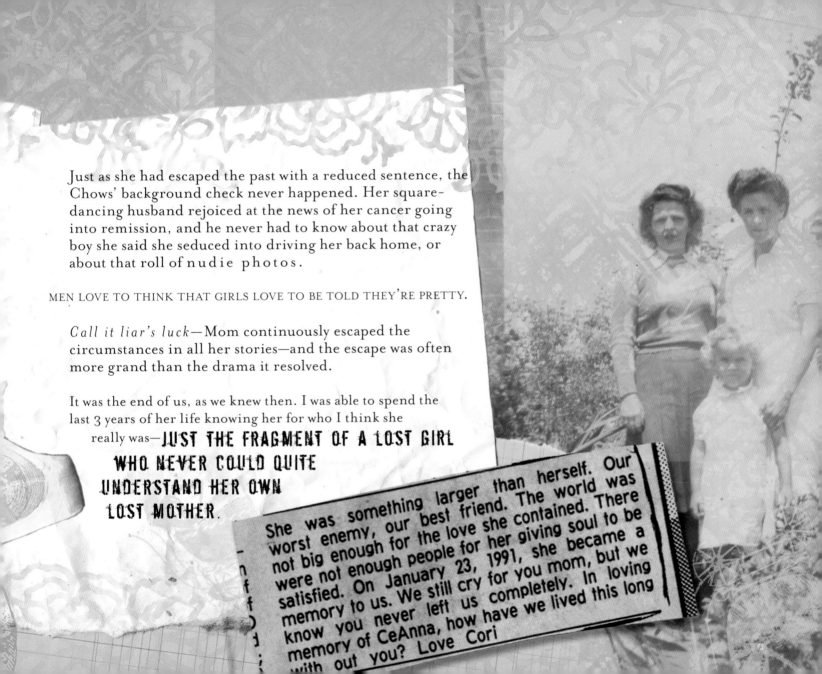

Just as she had escaped the past with a reduced sentence, the Chows' background check never happened. Her square-dancing husband rejoiced at the news of her cancer going into remission, and he never had to know about that crazy boy she said she seduced into driving her back home, or about that roll of n u d i e p h o t o s.

MEN LOVE TO THINK THAT GIRLS LOVE TO BE TOLD THEY'RE PRETTY.

Call it liar's luck—Mom continuously escaped the circumstances in all her stories—and the escape was often more grand than the drama it resolved.

It was the end of us, as we knew then. I was able to spend the last 3 years of her life knowing her for who I think she really was—JUST THE FRAGMENT OF A LOST GIRL WHO NEVER COULD QUITE UNDERSTAND HER OWN LOST MOTHER.

She was something larger than herself. Our worst enemy, our best friend. The world was not big enough for the love she contained. There were not enough people for her giving soul to be satisfied. On January 23, 1991, she became a memory to us. We still cry for you mom, but we know you never left us completely. In loving memory of CeAnna, how have we lived this long with out you? Love Cori

TAKING THE TEST

There were two whole weeks where I fretted, where I paced holes and wrung my red, NO-OTHER-PLAN hands. Two weeks where a single, 75-watt incandescent cloud hung above my furrowed face—and the answer of who I might and might not be was just beyond it, none-the-less blinding.

HE DIDN'T SHOW THE FIRST TIME, and I was out of shots and sorts. *They had stopped calling.* Fourteen whole days of no letters, no phone calls, and no answers—just owls in trees.

I SHOULD HAVE LIED, DAMN ME! DID SHE TEACH ME NOTHING?

and when
he called (*well, she called*—WELL, THEY CALLED) . . .

we got back on the crookedest of all tracks, where I'd passively poke a soft spot, then sink in the tie—and he'd constrict, console, and confuse. No trains a-rollin'. No forward march. No quick-and-easy get it over with, this won't hurt a bit.

Two or so weeks after David Hans Schnabel
didn't show up was when he did show up.

It was an out of the blue, last minute,
either now or never, here's my chance,
come on over sorta thing.

I said okay to myself.
I said, are you sure, girl?
I said, I'm going to know this
week, and what if I just don't want
to know after all?

What if he is my Dad and I have to bury
David Crooks? That second grave is
supposed to be for me. There's a man
coming over who could kill my father—
maybe I shouldn't answer the door.

What if he is my Dad
and I have to live with
the truth of this lie
again? *What if he is
my Dad and I have to
add 2 more strangers
to the list of siblings
that I don't know and
have to get to know,
and have to ache and
grieve over the loss of
time with and the loss
of time without?*

Carla called in the early afternoon. She said they were running errands.
She said they were thinking about coming out my way.
She said they wanted to know if I'd be around.

"Yeah, I'll be around."

cori 7/69

just found

So that leaves me.
With owls in my trees,
with a dead father
and a living one,
holding peaches,
apples, and my
mother's beloved lies.

I AM THE LAST OF
THE DANGLING HEADS.

**I AM HER
SEVENTH MISTAKE.**

The old house said that back at the end of
'69, that same foster family got a call again,
and they did what they thought was right, and
sought to bring back together what was left.

BABY #7

We lived the most time with Mom

**We, the last 3,
had been found alone.**
Child Services had been called.
We had been placed, 2, and then 1.

After a time, Bob and Cindy were released
to the care of our great-grandmother.
But they wouldn't let her take me.
She was much too old to care for a baby.
Peter and the twins' family tried, but it
involved bureaucracies and crossing states.

TOO MUCH RED TAPE.

The fate line.
I paid $10 to a fortune-teller once.
She said it ran deep through my hand and up to my
middle finger. She said when it does this, it is called
a GOD LINE. She said those few who have it are gifted
with GOD'S *innate permission* to
choose their own fate.

My Mom came back and said she had left us with a
baby sitter. That baby sitter must have disappeared.

"Give me back my baby."

Somehow things just happen the way they happen,
people do the things they do, and all that is done is done.
The wrist of my great-grandmother's house is tired,
yet she carries the past of my mother's children—STILL.

4 AND 20 BLACKBIRDS

When someone you've been waiting the last 14 years
for makes a left-hand turn onto your street,
you can hear the sound of the blinker.

When someone who holds the answers to your life
in his blood cells closes the door to his car, your heart skips.
Then slams shut.

When someone who is your very last chance,
who is your only true link to an uncertain beginning,
takes a step onto your wooden staircase,
your chest heaves with each footfall and your body
rocks with each knock, b a c k a n d f o r t h.

KNOCK, KNOCK, KNOCK.
And when I finally did open the door, I knew that he just couldn't be, that there was no possible way, and it suddenly became clear—and it suddenly became nice to see them.

"Hey, Little Sister," he said, like he always did.

Carla was small to my tall, pink to my orange, and her eyes were dark like the earth, while mine are dark with my mother's gray-blue storms. They rest in me, content with what I see—
this girl is not my sister, no.

"You look like Kimmy."
She reaches as she shows me pictures.

I know that I don't.

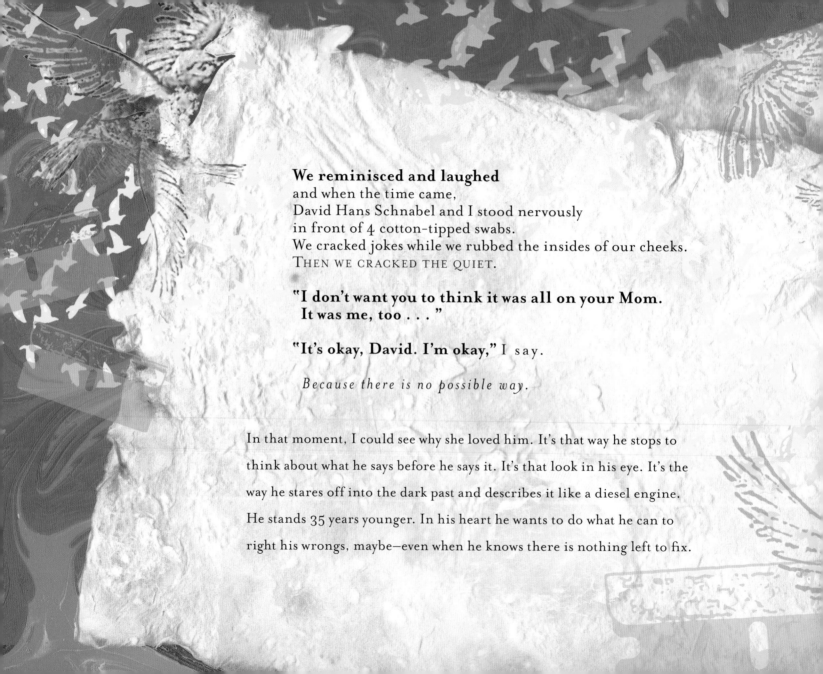

We reminisced and laughed
and when the time came,
David Hans Schnabel and I stood nervously
in front of 4 cotton-tipped swabs.
We cracked jokes while we rubbed the insides of our cheeks.
THEN WE CRACKED THE QUIET.

**"I don't want you to think it was all on your Mom.
It was me, too . . . "**

"It's okay, David. I'm okay," I say.

Because there is no possible way.

In that moment, I could see why she loved him. It's that way he stops to

think about what he says before he says it. It's that look in his eye. It's the

way he stares off into the dark past and describes it like a diesel engine.

He stands 35 years younger. In his heart he wants to do what he can to

right his wrongs, maybe—even when he knows there is nothing left to fix.

Eyes as black as pools.
Just like Mom's.

He nervously made a point of showing me
some photos he had kept in his wallet.

Me at 6. Me at 9. Me at 16. My graduation photo.
On the back of one, it appeared that he'd written:
"Aunt so-and-so's daughter."
He said he didn't know why that was there.

Then we ate pie.

THE RESULTS

STATEMENT OF RESULTS:
"Alleged relationship
is not excluded."

*When I read the results, I was alone.
I had promised myself that I'd wait,
but I couldn't.*

"BASED ON THE DNA ANALYSIS, THE ALLEGED
FATHER, DAVID H. SCHNABEL, CANNOT BE
EXCLUDED AS THE BIOLOGICAL
FATHER OF THE CHILD,
CORINA C. CROOKS,
BECAUSE THEY SHARE GENETIC MARKERS."

I accessed the results online. I had a secret code.
I had nothing to hold in my hands. Nothing to touch, nothing to tear.

"OF THE GENETIC IDENTITY SYSTEMS TESTED, 15 OF 15 MATCH
(99.989309288572% OF THE CAUCASIAN-AMERICAN MALE POPULATION
IS EXCLUDED FROM THE POSSIBILITY OF BEING THE BIOLOGICAL FATHER)."

**I read it over and over, hoping that I was missing something,
hoping that I didn't understand it correctly.**

Southwest Biotechnology and Informatics Center
Genetic Testing Laboratory
Las Cruces, New Mexico
Toll Free: (866) 633-6295

Results of DNA Analysis

<ORIGINAL REPORT IN COLOR>

Client Identification:		Corina Crooks						
Sample Source:				OID:	L04-10079		Report Release Date:	October 2004 NLB ANA INV2+ Page 1 of
Name:		Father (Alleged)		Child		Mother		
Race:		David H. Schnabel		Corina C. Crooks (Focus)		(Not Tested)		
Date Collected:		Caucasian-American		Caucasian-American				
		October 2004		October 2004				

STR Locus	Allele Range	Alleles Called		Alleles Called		Alleles Called		Exclusion Status*	Direct Index	Column Not Used
D3S1358	(12 - 20)									
TH01	(4 - 13.3)	17	18	15	18			OK		
D21S11	(24 - 38)	9.3	9.3	15	18			OK		
D18S51	(8 - 27)	30	31.2	6	7			OK		
Penta E	(5 - 24)	15	17	29	31.2			OK		
D5S818	(7 - 16)	11	17	7	17			OK	1.130	
D13S317	(7 - 15)	10	13					OK	1.561	
D7S820	(6 - 14)	11		10	11			OK	2.867	
D16S539	(5 - 15)	9	11	10	12			OK		
CSF1PO	(6 - 15)	11		9	11			OK	2.457	
Penta D	(2.2 - 17)	10	11					OK	12.500	
Amelogenin	(XX - XY)	13		10	11			OK	1.585	
vWA	(10 - 22)	Male (XY)		10	12			OK	2.766	
D8S1179	(7 - 18)	16	18	Female (XX)				OK	3.512	
TPOX	(6 - 13)	13	15	16	17			OK	0.833	
FGA	(16 - 46.2)	8		13				N/A	N/A	
NOT USED		23	25	8				OK	1.098	
NOT USED				21	25			OK	1.578	
NOT USED								OK	1.966	
NOT USED								OK	4.095	
NOT USED										
NOT USED										
NOT USED										

Laboratory Batch Number:	42873100A1	

Statement of Results: Alleged relationship is not excluded.   Notable Events: Exclusions-None; Infrequent Events-None. See COMMENTS section for additional information.

Based on the DNA analysis, the alleged Father, David H. Schnabel, cannot be excluded as the biological Father of the Child, Corina C. Crooks, because they share genetic markers. Of the genetic identity systems tested, 15 of 15 match, (99.989309288572% of the Caucasian-American male population is excluded from the possibility of being the biological Father. Analyses, with the exception of sample collection, were conducted in accordance with the relationship is indicated below, as compared with an untested, unrelated Caucasian-American male. Analyses, with the exception of sample collection, were conducted in accordance with the Standards for PCR DNA analysis set forth by the American Association of Blood Banks, (AABB).

Statistical Results:

Combined Direct Index   352,7..

Prior Probability   0.50   ....Probability =   99.999716544906%

.........Statistical Constant

Comments:

For legal and/or custody cases documentation of Informed Consent Notification and Sample Chain of Custody are included with this report using the ABI PRISM® 3100 Genetic Analyzer and analyzed with GeneScan® and GenoTyper® Software. "Exclusion" http://www.gtdna.com/interpretation.html < for a detailed explanation concerning the interpret...

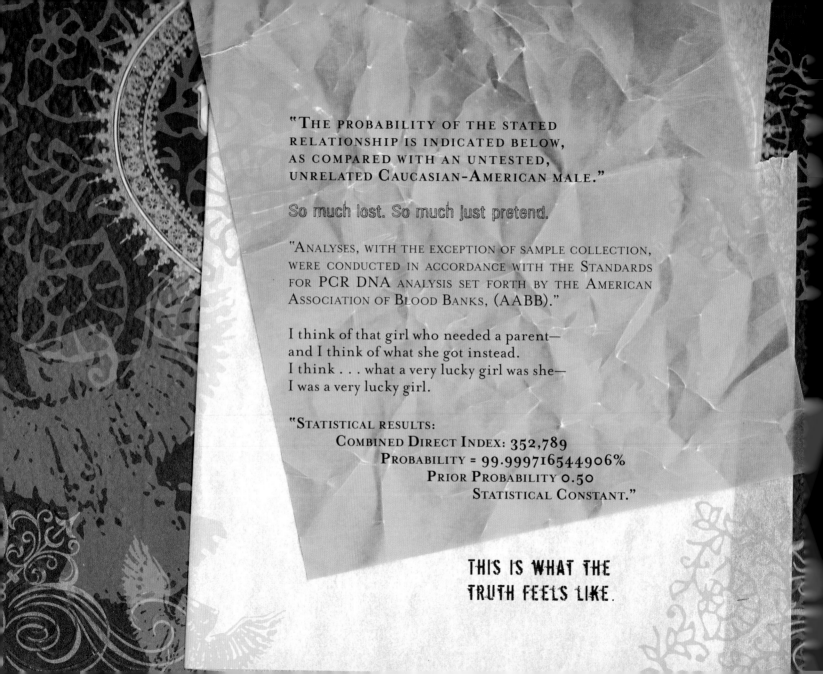

"The probability of the stated
relationship is indicated below,
as compared with an untested,
unrelated Caucasian-American male."

So much lost. So much just pretend.

"Analyses, with the exception of sample collection,
were conducted in accordance with the Standards
for PCR DNA analysis set forth by the American
Association of Blood Banks, (AABB)."

I think of that girl who needed a parent—
and I think of what she got instead.
I think . . . what a very lucky girl was she—
I was a very lucky girl.

"Statistical results:
   Combined Direct Index: 352,789
      Probability = 99.999716544906%
         Prior Probability 0.50
            Statistical Constant."

THIS IS WHAT THE
TRUTH FEELS LIKE.

BORN

My Mom said that when I was born, David Crooks took one look at me and knew I was his.

She said he named me *Corina* after a BOB DYLAN cover of an old Blind Lemon Jefferson song. She said he took me *everywhere he went,* never missing a chance to show off his little girl. She said he put my crib in their room so he could look after me through the night.

My Mom said the day he crashed his VW on Grayson Road, they had been fighting. He came home from the sugar plant and stuck his hard hat in the door to test her mood. *She threw it back at him.*

201

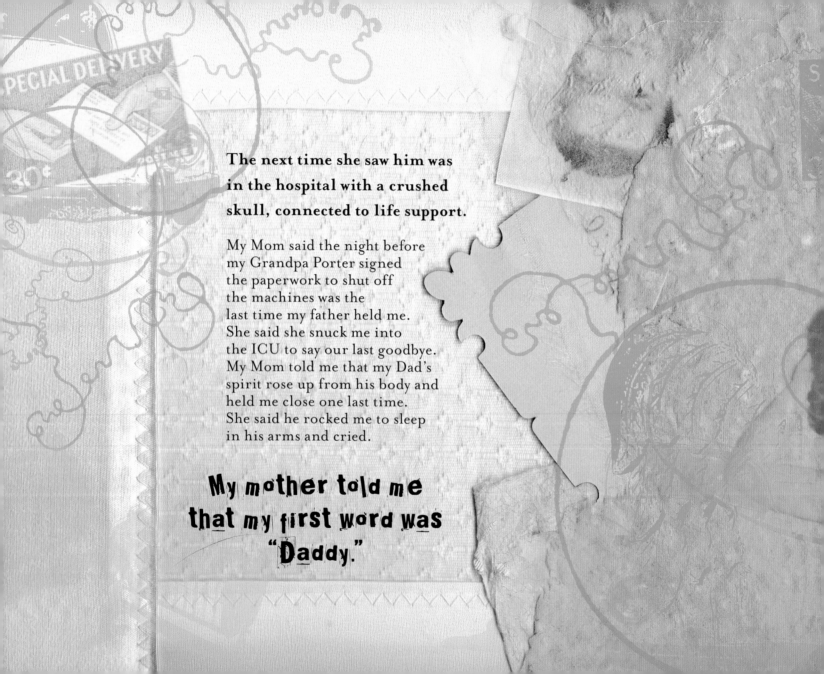

The next time she saw him was
in the hospital with a crushed
skull, connected to life support.

My Mom said the night before
my Grandpa Porter signed
the paperwork to shut off
the machines was the
last time my father held me.
She said she snuck me into
the ICU to say our last goodbye.
My Mom told me that my Dad's
spirit rose up from his body and
held me close one last time.
She said he rocked me to sleep
in his arms and cried.

My mother told me
that my first word was
"Daddy."

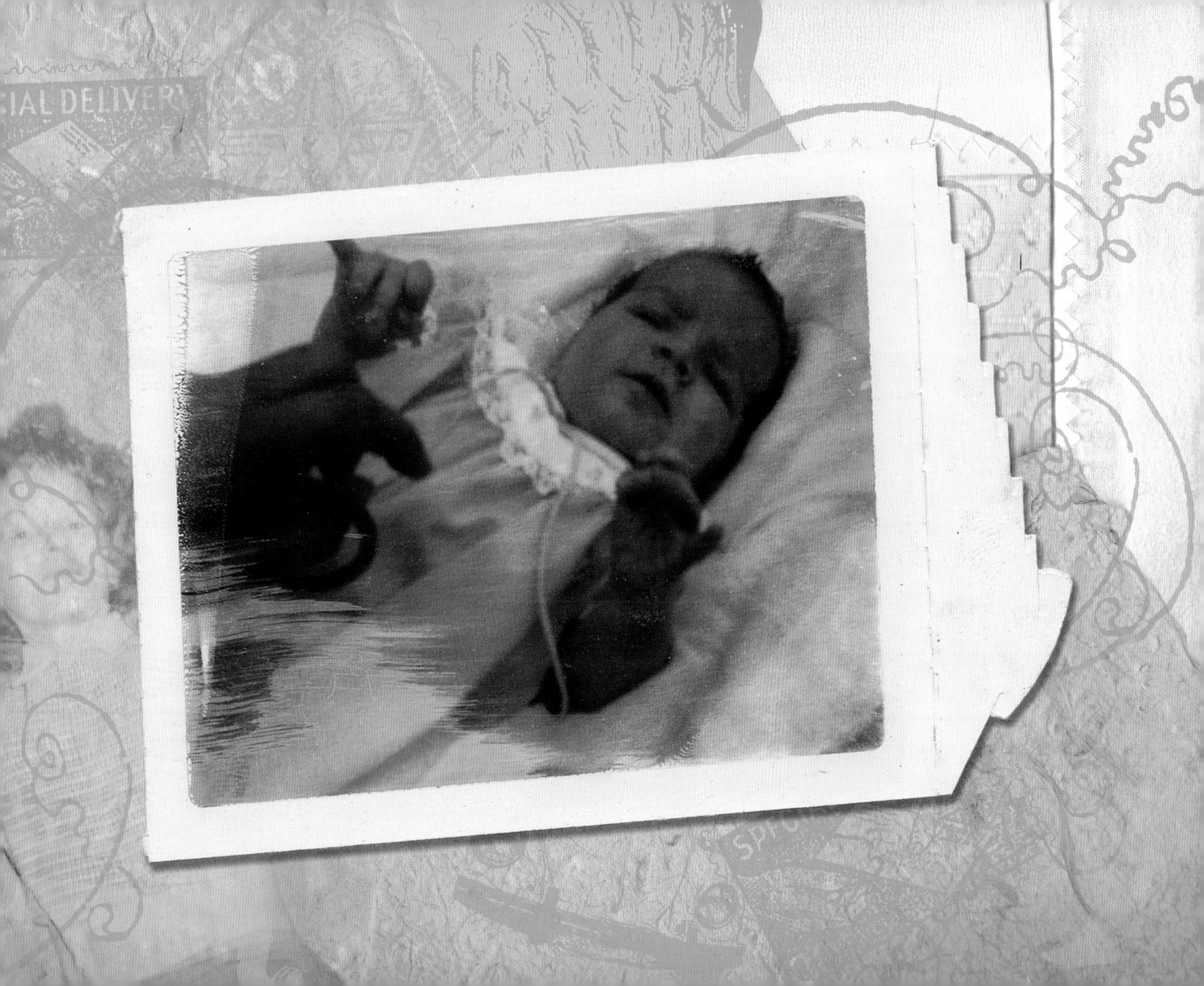
IAL DELIVERY

Acknowledgments

Thank you to every single person who read
and supported "A Gag Reflex."
Thanks to the brothers and sisters who understood my journey.
Thank you, David Crooks.

Dave Ferrin, the walking dictionary, thanks for watching the kids while I stared at the wall. Dennis Radonich and Carla Jourdan, thanks for the web support. Thanks to Bambouche, of the Vanguard Squad, for reminding me about artistic integrity. Literary agent Michelle Brower, thank you for your honesty, your belief in me, and your hard work. Thanks to the designer for her sensitivity and patience. Thank you to Seal Press for supporting women's voices everywhere.

"DNA Test Instructions," pages 1 & 2, GTL, Southwest Biotechnology and Informatics Center, NMSU. Reprinted courtesy of Dr. Peter Lammers.

Photo credit to Susan LeRoy Stewart and David Ferrin for "Baby #5".

A BIG THANKS AND ACKNOWLEDGEMENT IS MADE FOR PERMISSION TO REPRINT THE FOLLOWING MATERIAL:

All backgrounds, paintings, silkscreens and collages assembled by Domini Dragoone.

All other photographs, artwork, letters, and ephemera appear courtesy of the author:

Believing in myself has been one of the hardest things I have ever done—and this adventure was my attempt to find a me to believe in.

All the people in this book once existed and some still do. In the case of my siblings, I have decided to change their names and in one or two cases, photos. Discovering what one's truth is—is a personal quest. May they have peace and privacy for their own adventures.

CREDITS

Body text is Mrs. Eaves. All other
fonts were created by Eduardo Recife,
http://www.misprintedtype.com

"Love," c. 1979,
Roy Croft, (1907-1973).

"If you sprinkle when
you tinkle, be a sweetie,
wipe the seatie,"
Author unknown.

Every effort has been made to locate current copyright
holders in order to acquire permission for reprint.
Please contact publisher with attribution information.
Error or omissions will be corrected in subsequent editions.

SELECTED TITLES FROM
Seal Press

For more than thirty years, Seal Press has published groundbreaking books. By women. For women. Visit our website at www.sealpress.com. Check out the Seal Press blog at www.sealpress.com/blog.

The Chelsea Whistle: A Memoir, by Michelle Tea. $15.95, 1-58005-239-8. In this gritty, confessional memoir, Michelle Tea takes the reader back to the city of her childhood: Chelsea, Massachusetts—Boston's ugly, scrappy little sister and a place where time and hope are spent on things not getting any worse.

Rockabye: From Wild to Child, by Rebecca Woolf. $15.95, 1-58005-232-0. The coming-of-age story of a rock 'n' roll party girl who becomes unexpectedly pregnant, decides to keep the baby, and discovers motherhood on her own terms.

Fucking Daphne: Mostly True Stories and Fictions, edited by Daphne Gottlieb. $14.95, 1-58005-235-5. An erotic collection of stories, all centered on the fictional character "Daphne", that blurs the line between fact and fantasy.

Hellions: Pop Culture's Rebel Women, by Maria Raha. $15.95, 1-58005-240-1. Maria Raha, author of *Cinderella's Big Score,* analyzes women ranging from Marilyn Monroe to the reality TV stars of the twenty-first century in an effort to redefine the notion of female rebellion.

Cinderella's Big Score: Women of the Punk and Indie Underground, by Maria Raha. $17.95, 1-58005-116-2. A tribute to the transgressive women of the underground music scene, who not only rocked as hard as the boys, but also tested the limits of what is culturally acceptable—even in the anarchic world of punk.

Real Girl Real World: A Guide to Finding Your True Self, by Heather M. Gray and Samantha Phillips. $15.95, 1-58005-133-2. In this fun and essential guide, real girls share their experiences, showing that there's no one "right" way to navigate the twisting road of adolescence.